REPRINTED FROM THE TRANSACTIONS OF THE
BUCHAN FIELD CLUB, 1907.

FOLK-SONG IN BUCHAN.

BY

GAVIN GREIG, M.A., F.E.I.S.,

WHITEHILL, NEW DEER.

PETERHEAD:
P SCROGIE, "BUCHAN OBSERVER" PRINTING WORKS
1907.

REPRINTED FROM THE TRANSACTIONS OF THE
BUCHAN FIELD CLUB, 1906.

FOLK-SONG IN BUCHAN.

BY

GAVIN GREIG, M.A.,
NEW DEER.

PETERHEAD:
P. SCROGIE, "BUCHAN OBSERVER" PRINTING WORKS.
1906.

FOLK-SONG IN BUCHAN.

BY

GAVIN GREIG, M.A.

THE subject of Folk-Song is now attracting a good deal of attention. The absolute desire to know would of course send workers into this field as it does into other fields of investigation ; but there are other influences at work. The ever-widening outlook of modern culture, its transcendental reach and strain tend to fatigue the mind and even to daunt the soul ; and people are fain at times to turn aside for relief to the simpler forms of art where the programme is narrower and more clearly defined, and the utterance is marked by the directness of primitive feeling. For the musician in particular folk-song fulfils these conditions of relief and respite. Further, when it is found that the wildings of art we are in search of are fast passing into the limbo of forgotten things, there is added to the quest a certain element of urgency.

These considerations, however, are hardly sufficient to justify one in calling the attention of the Buchan Field Club to this subject of Folk-Song. Has it any word for us as a body of workers striving to read the story of Buchan? We think that it has. The field of local Folklore has already been to some extent explored, and with interesting results. The contiguous area of Folk-Song is likely to reward similar attention. A good deal has been done to trace the evolution of the Buchan man on the physical side ; but our picture of him cannot be complete till we take into account the emotional side of his nature. It is here that Folk-Song comes to our aid. Emotion in its ordinary and undisciplined manifestations hardly admits of appraisement, but when it receives artistic statement and presentation, even though the art-form employed be unambitious and its technique elementary, we begin to have material for some estimate of the general character of the feelings that now find expression as well as of their range and intensity.

This is the direct lesson of Folk-Song ; but incidentally we learn much more. We get light thrown on the social life of the people—their occupations and interests, their amusements and recreations ; while in the incidents and situations that have prompted and inspired the rustic muse local history may achieve record, or at least receive illustration. Further still, in our folk-songs the vocabulary and idiom of local speech, braced and quickened for its lyric task, may be studied to good and fruitful purpose. Nor is all this a detached and isolated field of investigation. It connects at every point with the world beyond "the bonnie Buchan borders." Our folk-song like our language has endless affinities, and together they become twin handmaids of ethnology.

One overt sign of the growing interest in folk-song is the formation quite recently of the Folk-Song Society. The official positions are filled by some of our leading musicians, and research is being industriously prosecuted by a number of experts. The results have amazed the workers. It used to be generally taken for granted that there was hardly such a thing as traditional folk-songs in South Britain. Now hundreds are being found in those rural districts that have been tapped. Ireland too has just started a Folk-Song Society.

There are signs that the movement is spreading to Scotland. It may seem somewhat strange that our southern neighbours should be leading the way in this work; but there are reasons for this. Folk-song has had a different history in the two countries. In England music has all along had a recognised place as one of the arts, and its composers have furnished the people with a more ambitious type of song than the ordinary traditional ditty. In Scotland, until lately at least, there has been practically nothing of this kind. Speaking generally, it may be said that only in the instrumental forms, Strathspey and Reel, has creative musical work been done north of the Tweed. As far as vocal music is concerned the people have had to be content with their own traditional minstrelsy. From that they have never been drawn away. They have kept the old-time tunes, selecting, adapting, improving at times; while the words have been largely rewritten by their best lyric poets. The intrusion of a certain amount of alien material into both departments was inevitable, but may be ignored. In this way has arisen that unique body of minstrelsy of which we are all so justly proud. English folk-song has received no such attention. It has never come to the surface, but has crept along among the lower ranks of a dull peasantry, unnoted by the more intelligent classes, until the very fact of its existence has had in a sense to be discovered. Over this discovery our English friends are naturally jubilant. And further, finding a family resemblance between their own old songs and ours, they are beginning to maintain that both derive from the same source and that ours came north with the language. This is no doubt true in a sense. Yet it hardly affects the credit of old Scotland. Our minstrelsy did come north—in originals and types, charged with certain aims and tendencies; and in the lower strata of our northern folk-song, where evolution has not proceeded so very far, we find affinities with English folk-song that clearly argue for both streams a common source. But what we call Scottish Song—our accepted and standard minstrelsy, is something very different from English folk-song. The origin may be again the same; but the northern stream has travelled a good way during the centuries, and, in the main, in the right direction. Scotland may not have created her minstrelsy, but she has made it three parts her own by putting into it the best of her heart and life. If then the Southerner after the lapse of centuries digs from the ground his talent still one and unimproved, while his northern neighbour can show his grown to ten and bright and beautiful with loving use, it matters little to say now that both started with an equal endowment from the same original source.

If in the field of folk-song England is setting herself to reap a belated harvest, Scotland may be reminded that she has still a considerable aftermath to secure, and that it behoves her to be up and doing. It may occur to some to wonder why after so much has been done in the way of collecting our traditional minstrelsy there should remain any considerable body of it to collect. Some explanation may be offered. In former days collectors of folk-songs had a practical purpose in view. They wanted songs that could go into printed collections and that would be taken up and sung. The words had to reach a certain standard of merit; and, when they failed to reach that standard, the song had to be set aside, however good the tune might be. Burns, when he found a good tune with indifferent words, would rewrite the verses; but the ordinary collector, not having the necessary literary faculty for such an achievement, would have to let the whole song go by the board. Sometimes the music was the stumbling-block, not because it wanted merit, but because it happened to be in some ancient mode with which the singer's ear was growing somewhat unfamiliar.

The programme and aims of the present-day collector of folk-songs are vastly wider and more thorough-going than those that used to guide the chance worker in this field in days gone by. The worker of to-day ignores nothing that is traditional. For him the humblest ditty has significance, but the main consideration that guides him is this—He finds that, although the words of our traditional ditties are usually poor enough, the melodies to which they are set are almost always good; in many cases fine; in cases not a few superior to all except the very best of the airs in our standard collection of Scottish Song.

How stands it now with us in this matter of folk-song? Scotland is too big a word for us as yet. Let us confine our attention meantime to our own north-eastern angle. We are usually spoken of as a land apart—Boeotian, bucolic. We are supposed to be unemotional to a degree. There may be some truth in all this; but we are entitled to make one or two claims. To our Scottish anthology Buchan has contributed two lyrics of the very first rank—" Logie o' Buchan," and "Tullochgorum." With these I have already dealt in a paper on "Two Buchan Songs" contributed to the Transactions of the Club. Besides these masterpieces of lyrical achievement we can claim two or three songs of the second rank; and altogether our reputation in the field of lyrism is higher than that of any other district north of the Tay. Still better do we show in the matter of attention to traditional song and ballad. Our two champions here are Peter Buchan and Dean Christie—the former as a collector of the words of our old ballads, the latter as a collector chiefly of the airs; and each in his own domain may be confidently backed against all comers north of the Tweed. Peter Buchan and his works have been ably and exhaustively treated by Mr J. A. Fairley, Edinburgh, in a valuable paper contributed to Vol. VII. of the Club's Transactions. The redoubtable Peter remains the prince of ballad collectors. His *Gleanings of Scarce Old Ballads* (1825), his *Ancient Ballads and Songs of the North of Scotland* (1828), together with the Chap Books which he issued from time to time, represent an amount of work in the way of collecting, editing, and printing our old ballads, that gives him a place and reputation in this particular field quite beyond serious challenge. Some recent critics like Mr T. F. Henderson are pretty hard on Peter Buchan. They have scant faith in his work. Buchan we know was himself misled at times; and he in turn doubtless misleads us now and again. The ethics of collecting and editing was pretty elastic in those days, and Peter could hardly be expected to anticipate the severer standard of a later generation. But he does not appear to have been a sinner above and beyond other collectors and editors of his own day and generation. He seems to be at least as reliable as Hogg, and much more so than Allan Cunningham. In any case only those who have themselves worked in the area which he explored are in a position to judge of the value of the results of his research; and those who possess this qualification are very far from endorsing the criticism which characterises Peter's collection as in considerable measure "a mere farrago of unauthentic doggerel."

Dean Christie set himself to do for the airs of our northern ballads what Peter Buchan had already done for the words. His father, William Christie of Monquhitter (circ. 1778-1849), was a dancing master, violinist, and composer. About 1821 he published a collection of Reels, most of which were composed or arranged by himself. He also set himself to collect old inedited ballad airs. By and by his son joined in the work, and at the time of the old man's death the collection amounted to nearly 250. These the two had arranged and harmonised as an Album of Ballad Music for private use. More unpublished airs were afterwards discovered by the Dean, and the collection was ultimately published as "Traditional Ballad Airs," arranged from copies procured in the counties of Aberdeen, Banff, and Moray, in two quarto volumes (1876 and 1881). The collection is by far the largest ever published in Scotland. Christie who had been Dean of the United Diocese of Moray, Ross, and Caithness, since 1861, died at Bellie near Fochabers in 1885.

Before one can judge fairly of any work, one must know what ends the author proposed to himself, what purpose he meant his work to serve. It is pretty evident that what Dean Christie aimed at in his *Traditional Ballad Airs* was to keep alive the old popular minstrelsy of the north-east, and to extend its vogue by introducing it to a larger and better public. To secure these ends he appears to have judged certain things to be necessary. The words of the ballads had to be unimpeachable. When the traditional verses were of very poor literary quality or offended against good taste, he substituted other lyrics. The music, however, gave him much more trouble than the words did. One difficulty was inseparable from the situation. Traditional tunes get changed in passing from singer to singer. The variations are frequently very considerable. The Dean when collecting had often got two or more versions of a tune. What was he to do now when only one could go into the book? He might have selected what he considered the best version and printed that. This plan did not appear to him to meet the needs of the case; and he set himself to make, by some kind of eclectic process, one version from the different copies before him. Then he had to bring the music in line, as far as possible, with conventional ideas. He seems to have taken it for granted that a ballad air should have two strains. When he found only one strain—and this we know must have been his general experience, he had to supply the defect somehow. Perseverance—and ingenuity, came to his rescue. He tells us that in some cases he discovered that the two strains had got divorced. The first strain would be sung in Aberdeenshire, and the second in Banff-shire, and *vice versa*. The worthy Dean was doubtless acting in good faith in piecing together what he took to be *disjecta membra*. All the same we think that he must have been mistaken. It is about as certain as anything can well be that our old ballad airs had originally but one strain, corresponding to the ordinary quatrain to which they were sung. When we do come across a second strain we may be pretty sure that it is the work of some later hand; and we shall find it as a rule merely a free dishing up again of the first strain. Remembering how the versions of a traditional tune which have been got in different localities may vary, we can easily conceive the Dean taking for a second strain of a tune what was merely another version of it. The two would be sufficiently alike to suggest a structural relation of some kind or other, and yet sufficiently unlike to prevent them from being taken as mere variants of one and the same original tune. Only occasionally, however, would the Dean have the good fortune thus to discover what he considered the missing member, and often, we fear, for his second strain must he have been thrown pretty much on his own resources. Yet the task of supplying what was wanted was by no means a serious one, nor needed it disturb the conscience very much. Invention was hardly required; for new material there was scarcely any demand. One or two very simple devices sufficed. The repetition, for instance, of one bit of the tune in the higher octave, and of another bit *in loco*, with a few connecting notes, was enough to satisfy the arranger and his clients that they were not just going over the same ground again. Once more, Dean Christie judged that pianoforte accompaniments were necessary if the songs were to become acceptable to the better public whom he had in view. In this of course he was right; but he unwisely attempted to combine the instrumental with the vocal part. Neither in this way gets justice. It would have been much better to take half the airs, and thus get room for a separate pianoforte score into which some variety, colour, and interest could be thrown, while the voice part was at the same time more readily readable.

Our programme as collectors and students of folk-song differs considerably from that of Dean Christie. We do not overlook the practical aspect of the matter. We should like to see the best of our traditional folk-songs revived and sung all over the country. They might well replace a good deal of the vocal music that is now in vogue. To fit them for being taken up and sung, a bit of arranging and editing will be necessary. Meanwhile, however, our main purpose is, in a broad sense, scientific. We want to understand folk-song and to read its message. For this end we must, to begin with, collect as large a body of folk-songs as possible, in order that we may have material for generalisation. Then we must see that we have the undiluted article. We must in collecting take just what we find, and, in our record, give exactly what we get. Hence it comes that Dean Christie's work is of comparatively little use to us. We never know how much of the editor we have in any of the songs which he prints. We know we have always some, and often, we fear, a good deal. Thirty of his originals faithfully given would have been worth immeasurably more than the whole three hundred airs which he has "arranged and harmonised." We do not blame the Dean. He acted according to his light and his conception of what was wanted. He was not to know how the subject of folk-song would be taken up a generation later. At the same time it will be matter for deep and lasting regret among students of folk-song that it did not occur to him to use otherwise than he did the great opportunity which he had—an opportunity which in the nature of things can never recur to be embraced by any other worker in this field.

In the matter of attention to folk-song we claim that our north-eastern angle has during the past century done exceedingly well ; and it is gratifying to find that in the folk-song revival which the new century has brought our district is once more well to the front. To the New Spalding Club belongs the credit of re-directing attention to the subject. Honoured with instructions from the Club to prospect and report as to the feasibility of making a collection of " the older popular music of the north-east," I have for some considerable time been engaged in investigating the subject, and as a result of this preliminary survey have been able to report that the project is both feasible and well worth carrying out, and have recommended that it be proceeded with. The Club has accepted the recommendation, and has decided to place on its programme of works to be issued a volume on the Folk-Music of the North-east. Undertaking the work, I have asked that the Rev. James B. Duncan, M A., Lynturk, be associated with me as joint-editor, and to this the Club has cordially assented.

Another very encouraging sign of the times falls to be gratefully recorded. I have received from the Carnegie Trust Research Scheme a grant in aid of our folk-song work. The broad and enlightened views which seem to guide the Trustees in the administration of the scheme deserve the warmest recognition. The grant is very welcome and valuable as helping to provide the sinews of war for our folk-song campaign. Not less important is the moral effect of the recognition thus accorded to this new line of research work.

Narrowing our view meantime to our own district, we should like to take this opportunity of saying something about folk-song as we find it in Buchan at the present moment, with a view to creating increased interest in the work of collecting, and in the hope that we may succeed in enlisting the kind help of all who may be able in one way or another to further the enterprise. One cannot profess as yet to have gone over the field with any degree of thoroughness, but with the help of many kind and willing friends I have succeeded in getting together a pretty large and representative collection of Buchan folk-songs. And there have been other workers in this field of whose labours I am permitted to avail myself. Mr John Milne, Maud, one of our worthy vice-presidents, has made a special study of the words of our local ditties, gathering a large collection of characteristic specimens; while Mr George Riddell, one of the best musicians we have in this part of the country, has done the same by the tunes. Then my friend and collaborator, the Rev. Mr Duncan, while he has a wide and accurate knowledge of folk-song in all its bearings, claims special and intimate acquaintance with the folk-songs of Buchan, of which district indeed he is a distinguished native.

Though we take a definite area for our proposed survey we must ever carefully avoid the error of supposing that we can assign to it any definite body of native minstrelsy. We do indeed find a number of songs, the words of which are, or appear to be, of local origin; but even the most original of these will likely enough be found to be modelled on older ditties, which in some cases they have supplanted, while not a few have been localised by simply changing a name or an allusion. Still more are the old tunes common property—the fact in their case being more difficult to overlay. The collector must in the first instance take just what he finds. He receives everything with an open mind, and goes ahead, quite prepared for developments. These come thick and fast. As his collection grows he more and more discovers identities, always qualified of course by the variations that are inseparable from oral transmission; he discovers endless resemblances, affinities, imitations, echoes, until there is woven around him and his subject a web that threatens to strangle both. We do not wish to alarm people who may think of taking up the subject, but we think it well to warn them that folk-song is by no means the innocent simple thing it looks. It admits indeed of no delimitation either in a geographical or in a secular way, reaching forth ultimately to the ends of the earth, and back to primeval times. Its fountain-head cannot well be found; but it is something to know that its streams are racial.

Setting aside meanwhile, as far as may be possible, those wider issues, we would deal with traditional song as we find it in our own Buchan at the present hour. The matter of finding it demands some attention; for it may very easily be missed. In our rural districts long ago almost everybody sang or tried to sing. The standard of vocal attainment was low, and no accompaniments were needed. The occasions were always social, and criticism was mild and mutual. Around the ingle or in a barn where all were neighbours and cronies, nobody who could sing at all would hesitate to contribute his or her favourite ballad or ditty. Now-a-days we cultivate singing as an art, till as a rule in a company nobody will sing at all unless they can do it fairly well. And singers are taking up a different class of song—songs of more pretension and usually with pianoforte accompaniment. These changes have largely silenced our once vocal vales. The older people have pretty much ceased to sing the folk-songs of their youth, having long been taught to regard them as semi-barbarous compared with modern songs; while the younger generation hardly know the old-time minstrelsy at all. While this is the case generally over our rural areas, some exception must be made as regards the farm-servant class. They have been least affected by the changes in taste and practice which modern days have brought; and the ploughman song can still be heard sung by lusty lungs in the field or by the fireside. If it cannot quite be said to flourish it at least lives, and with vitality strong enough to keep the record open for the occasional addition of a new ditty in the old manner. Our ploughman lads, however, are rather shy of approach, and it needs a good deal of tact and resource to get at them and secure their minstrel treasures. In most cases indeed folk-songs have to be hunted for. Not even in our most remote districts do they assail one's ears. Nay, it would be possible for one to spend a lifetime even in Buchan and hardly know of their existence. It is to the older people, as a rule, that we must go if we want to learn about our traditional songs. Usually it is somewhat difficult to induce them to sing the old ditties. They are slow to believe that anyone—especially a musician—can be interested in these things; but, when they get reassured and well started, they generally become themselves interested in the quest, and will do their best to recall and sing the lilts of earlier days, and their memories are wonderfully good, although at times there may occur lacunae in their recollections of the words. This plan of going to oral and traditional sources marks the new folk-song movement. A good deal of the ink used by Ritson, Chappell, Glen, and others, in fighting over the question of the nationality of songs, might have been saved, had they depended less on the testimony of books and manuscripts, and gone more to oral and traditional sources for their information and for the material from which to construct their theories.

The contents of the rustic singer's wallet are usually somewhat mixed. He is not particularly discriminating, and from one source or another has picked up this thing and the next—old, middle-aged, and fairly new, although the bulk of his stock is distinctly native. To this kind of thing indeed his hereditary ear and taste seem to direct him. The alien elements that have crept into his stock we would seek to discard, although it is not easy drawing a hard and fast line.

We are dealing with songs. Now a song is a union of words and music. We cannot judge of the product aright without having both before us. Further, we should hear it actually sung. Very specially is this needed in the case of folk-songs, the rendering of which is traditional and characteristic. In dealing critically with a song, however, it is convenient, if not almost necessary, to begin by treating each part—words and music, separately. A few preliminary remarks, then, we would offer on these two heads. And these remarks must be very general. The field has as yet been far too imperfectly surveyed to admit of precise statement or to encourage confident opinion. Principles and categories must be kept wide and elastic; and when we presume to theorise, we must do it in a cautious and tentative way.

The mixed character which we have attributed to folk-song applies in a special way to the words. They differ markedly in origin, character, and history. A loose classification, however, is admissible, and may be so far helpful. We still have the old ballad, although it has in considerable measure lost its traditional character. Our old ballads indeed have received quite an extraordinary amount of attention. They have been collected, edited, printed, and annotated, with almost unexampled fulness; and they now occupy a definite and recognised place in poetic literature. The record has been practically closed and the last word said in Professor Child's great work, *English and Scottish Popular Ballads* (1882-98). The one regret that may be expressed in connection with the recent history of our ballads is that the text and the tunes have as a rule got divorced. The words are thus apt to be judged by purely literary canons. They must, however, be heard sung, and sung too in the traditional way, before their meaning and message can be duly appreciated. One sometimes wonders how many of our recent ballad editors ever heard them so rendered.

There is a kind of ballad which we frequently encounter, of more recent origin and of lower literary quality than the old heroic ballad. Many of these hail from England and some from Ireland, although the northern singer may have Scotticised the language to a greater or less extent. Some of them, of the "Jack Munro" type, may be fairly old, but most are of comparatively recent date. Quite a number are more or less martial in character, and belong to the period of the Napoleonic wars. They may be called ballads inasmuch as they are narrative, but they have parted with some of the most characteristic and best features of the older form. Some there are that quite obviously belong to the north. They appear as a rule to be the work of some humble rhymer, who is frequently himself also the hero of the tale. The theme too is humble—some local incident, pretty often of an unfortunate kind. Sentiment and reflection are conventional, with a tendency to the lugubrious. In the literary workmanship, such as it is, one seems to trace the influence of our metrical psalms and paraphrases. The poorer kind of these compositions are pretty much what the unconventional critic would call "strouds." Through this general lack of distinction these ballads have been mostly left in the keeping of local tradition. A specimen may be given by way of illustration. "Jock Scott" hails from central Buchan, and deals with incidents and characters belonging to the earlier part of last century.—

  Come all my friends both far and near,
   And listen to my song;
  I've penned it with a troubled mind,
   To hold me on-thought long.

  First time I saw my Mary
   Was in the month of May;
  Down by her father's dwelling
   I carelessly did stray.

  Upon her I did bend mine eye,
   But she ne'er looked behind;
  Her cheeks were blooming like a rose,
   I wished that she'd been mine.

Her father did a servant want ;
  With him I did agree ;
Six months with him then I was bound
  His servant for to be.

Jock and the daughter became lovers, and afterwards eloped.—

But then our sorrows did begin ;
  Her father did pursue,
And grieved was I to see his face,
  For he did her abuse.

He has set her on a horse,
  She's torn away from me ;
She stretchèd out her lily hand,
  For tears she could not see.

He has ta'en her back again,
  And sore it grievèd me ;
But she sent word just that same night
  That she would constant be.

They make another attempt a twelvemonth later and succeed.—

To Aberdeen we cheerily went,
  We soon got joinèd there ;
And home again we did return,
  And to them did declare.

Nine months we lived together,
  Love smiled between us twa,
When both inclined to go away
  To North America.

But now the hope of this is past,
  For forgery I am ta'en ;
And here I lie to wait my call,
  In the jail o' Aberdeen.

Her father he has put me here,
  I'm sure it was a shame,
The County Fiscal he has told
  That I did forge his name.

But innocent I'll plead of it,
  And never will deny ;
And if that I do justice get,
  I will them all defy.

The genesis of the song seems to have been different from that of the ballad. Although both in their final form represent an alliance between poetry and music, they started in different ways. The ballad began with the words. There was a desire to celebrate some heroic achievement—to hand down to memory some notable happening. The narration sought form, and looked about for support and enforcement. Rythm and rhyme offered their services. These would conciliate and impress the listener, and, as regards the reciter, would be a great aid to memory and delivery. The voice in reciting the rhymed chronicle that had been thus evolved would naturally assume intonation and inflection, and pass from chant to rudimentary melody, until an alliance between words and music—both of a somewhat primitive order—got established and confirmed. The words, however, always remained the chief partner in this alliance; and in this connection it is significant that modern editors of our old ballads have largely ignored the tunes to which they were sung.

The song seems to have had an original association with music. The starting-point was rhythmical movement with accompanying music —the dance, as a rule, in some form. An instrument might be used to begin with; but the human voice would tend to accompany and at times to replace the instrumental strains. As an aid to vocalisation and to indicate rhythmic grouping there would be extemporised a succession of suitable syllables. These might be at first meaningless, and this original kind of vocalise still remains in folk-song refrains; but there would be a natural transition to phrases and lines of actual words whose accentuation corresponded to the rhythm of the allied movements. In this way arose the nonsense verses which were originally sung to the dance—a kind of thing which is not unknown in our own day.—

> Can you dance the polka? Yes I can—
> Round and round with a nice young man, &c.

Even without music the sequences of movements which came natural to mother and child suggested the nursery rhyme with all its whimsicalities. Many of our old songs still show how they originated and were evolved. We have a line or a couplet expanded in one way or another into a quatrain as an impromptu to suit the rhythm of a tune—

> Green grows the rashes, O.

> Haud awa, bide awa,
> Haud awa frae me, Donald.

> Jenny dang, dang, dang,
> Jenny dang the weaver.

> We're a' noddin',
>   Nid, nid, noddin',
> And we're a' noddin'
>   At oor hoose at hame.

It may be, on the other hand, that certain collocations of words suggested a rhythmical structure for a tune. These impromptus, detached, inconsequential, whimsical, and even freakish, might through some chance association of ideas suggest a motive which would be afterwards worked out in a group of stanzas, with the original impromptu as a kind of chorus or refrain. Some of those old phrases and lines were doubtless meant to be enigmatical and suggestive, as can be seen from the way in which the idea understood to be conveyed in them has been worked out in certain old versions of the resultant songs. Much of Burns' work consisted in returning on the original germ and evolving it along other and better lines. And, in passing, one may venture the opinion that much of lyric trick and surprise has come from exploiting the chance associations of ideas discovered in those old vagabond impromptus. Concurrently with those primitive attempts at evolving the lyric would proceed another movement. Song would gradually part company with the dance and set up on its own account. With other kinds of motion of a less exacting and absorbing nature it still retained a certain measure of association. This is extensively illustrated in Celtic minstrelsy, as connected with the social life of the people. Not even with the dance, indeed, did Highland song part company. There was the "Port-a-beul," sung to verses more or less nonsensical by the maidens while their companions danced; the "Liuneags," sung by them in seasons both of work and diversion; the "Iorrums," sung by the men while rowing; and as each member of the rustic band left for ever the joys and sorrows of mortal life there was the sad "Coronach," sung by the mourners as they carried to the grave the body of their late comrade. The association of song with labour is further illustrated in Sailors' Chanties. Our seamen have certain ditties with which they accompany the particular tasks which they have to perform on board ship. These chanties, as they are called, help at once to regulate movements and to inspirit the men; and, as before, would appear to have originated in impromptus.

The evolution of the lyric as a literary form has not proceeded very far with the folk-songist. He is as an individual shy of self-revelation and does not care to "give himself away." He is prepared on occasion to exhibit a certain amount of exaltation, but he is too self-conscious to affect any great depth or refinement of feeling. Thus, even if left to himself, the folk-songist might be expected to keep his rustic muse well in hand and to impose on all its utterances a certain restraint. But he was not left to himself. Song in his little world was social. Things may be changing now, but in our rural communities long ago, as we have already said, practically everybody sang—

> On Fasten-e'en we had a rockin'
> To ca' the crack and weave our stockin',
> And there was muckle fun and jokin'
> Ye needna doubt;
> At length we had a hearty yokin'
> At sang about.

In such companies and on such occasions there was no professionalism—no thought of voice-culture, hardly any technique. Each one sang in his own way and as nature had endowed him. The words were so much more important than the tune that, so long as a singer had an acceptable lyric to declaim, it did not so much matter though his voice was poor and his execution faulty. The company all knew each other, and, as the outcome of many a happy turn at "sang about," each member of the circle had usually got identified with some particular song, which he had to sing on every occasion. Neither the singer nor his hearers ever tired of it. If song was thus social in its presentation and rendering, it was also largely communal as regards origin, material, and putting together. It had to represent the general lyric sense, satisfying the lyric ideals and aspirations of the community for whom it had become the main channel of emotional utterance. The body of song that had this necessary sanction and hall-mark had derived and grown rather than been produced. Origins could hardly be traced. The rustic singer did not go to books for his songs. He must pick them off somebody; must hear them rendered; must in short feel assured that they were songs already in the full and complete sense. Even when a song did appear to have taken a more or less definite beginning it was hardly a new and individual effort. The motive would be found to lie well within the recognised area of exploitation. The general framework was familiar. Vocable and idiom, entity and epithet, figure and phrase —all had been picked from the armoury of authentic folk-song ; the whole composition was in line with the general way of looking at things and of putting things. Of course a little freshness was welcome. If, however, the novelty was too pronounced it would by-and-by get reduced ; for, as a rule, everything that was outstanding in folk-song got touched up—or down, by the many hands through which it passed, until the product came to satisfy the general lyric sense and expectation. Sometimes we do come across a verse that stands well out from the context.—

> I can drink and no be drunk,
> I can fight and no be slain,
> I can court a neighbour's lass,
>   And aye be welcome to my ain.
>
> If a' were wrocht that's ta'en in hand,
>   And a' were peyed that's promised me,
> I'd gang again the gate I cam',
>   And a better laddie I wad be.

But, as if to familiarise ear and mind with the too pronounced deliverance and mitigate its surprise, verses like the above will frequently be found repeated in other songs. Another point falls to be noted as illustrating the communal origin and treatment of folk-song. Living folk-songs hardly ever appear to be distinctly old. If we were to treat them as original compositions we should be inclined to say, from internal evidence, that they had all been produced within the past century. But we know that they are not original compositions, and that the general continuity of folk-song has never been broken. The only explanation of the situation is that folk-song has always been, in a sense, kept up to date. New versions from time to time replace older ones. Even when the old songs were less drastically handled the archaic in them in thought and language, character and incident, came to be revised from time to time ; had to be, in fact, if the song was to remain a living and effective instrument of emotional expression. All this is done in an unobtrusive yet wholly inevitable way through the operation of the communal sense. The average rustic has not imagination enough to project himself into scenes and situations of a far-off day, which, while they profess to belong to his own particular world, ever and anon distract with their anomalies and anachronisms. He does not feel the same difficulty with the old heroic ballads, for the world into which they invite him is as far removed from his own world socially, and usually also geographically, as it is temporally.

Folk-song by a kind of social gravitation always seeks the lowest level, and keeps it. It is necessarily of the people and for the people, and all attempts to raise it are soon met by a certain invincible inertia, for it cannot transcend the average lyric sense and sanction of the plebs. Every attempt to give folk-song literary form and distinction fails beyond a certain point. Songs written for the people from the outside —the outside laterally or vertically, are pretty certain to fail. The new claimants to popular favour and acceptance simply do not "catch on." There is no critical storm raised over the business—no literary squabbles; for the folk-songist has no such word as literature in his vocabulary. He just knows what he wants to sing; and there is an end of it. He has his own anthology, and wants no exotics. His flowers must suit the climate and do without attention.—

> The flaunting flowers our gardens yield
> High sheltering woods and wa's maun shield;
> But thou beneath the random bield
>   O' clod or stane,
> Adorns the histie stibble field,
>   Unseen, alane.

Yes, your folk-songist knows what is what—knows his own mind; and if he wants the daisy, the broom, or the heather, you cannot get him to take to the rose or the lily. Absolute, instinctive, unreasoning confidence may be decried, but it is usually the final note of relative truth. And the folk-songist is right. His daisy, broom, and heather, are the best for *him*; and, if he cared to think of it, he could set his superior critics a fairly hard task to show that his wildings were not *per se* as perfect as the rose and the lily. If Scottish folk-song could have been raised Burns was the man to do it; but not even *he* succeeded. He has not given the people a new and higher type of folk-song; he has only reinforced and enriched in measureless degree a kind of song that, however it may all along have hung on the horizon, has never quite been folk-song. The rustic knows his Burns, and likes on occasion to hear his songs rendered by those who *can* sing them. But they are hardly for *him*. Like sunday clothes or best crockery they are too good for ordinary use. He will sing *about* Burns, but it must be in lays that have got the folk-song hall-mark—in ditties that have little literary kinship with the poet's own songs. Though he does not offer to sing

> Ye banks and braes and streams around
> The castle o' Montgomery;

he will throw all his heart into

> In green Caledonia there ne'er were twa lovers
> Sae enraptured and happy in each ither's arms,
> As Burns the sweet Bard and his dear Highland Mary,
> And fondly and sweetly he sang o' her charms.

And, although "There was a lad was born in Kyle" is not exactly in his line, he will declaim with infinite zest, "The Cottage where Robbie was born."

Passing from these more general considerations, we would deal with the particular literary qualities, such as they are, that are found in folk-song. When song brings poetry and music together the alliance thus established involves a compromise, a limitation of function and aim on both sides. Absolute music must be purely instrumental; and the highest forms of poetry refuse to be sung. In song the appeal is mainly to the feelings. Whatever in verses to be sung closely engages the intellect is a distraction and tends to weaken the effect. We cannot afford to be startled with point, or burdened with the task of diluting pregnancies. The meaning must be obvious and sufficiently well spaced out, combining with the music to produce an atmosphere with large and fairly even touch. Even in the Kunstlied, or Artistic Song, purely literary qualities must not obtrude. Still more does this veto apply to the Volkslied or Popular Song. True folk-song, however, does not tend to err in this respect. The communal sense to which we have already referred may be trusted to keep things right; but really there is comparatively little tendency to go wrong. The rustic singer is so far from hankering after literary effects that, so long as the general meaning is clear, he does not much trouble about details of any kind. He is, for example, no verbal critic. He will continue to sing words or phrases that are wrong or inept without ever appearing to notice that there is anything out of joint. This is partly due to the way in which songs are learned. The singer has not got them from a book; he has picked them up by ear from some other body, when mistakes are easily made or copied. The result is also due in some measure to the fact that the subordination of the intellect to which we have referred has grown a habit. There may be a dim impression that there is something strange or obscure about a word or phrase that is being sung, but the mental and critical faculties are too relaxed to attack the problem; and the oftener the song is sung the less inclination is there to examine the words in detail. Some rather strange instances could be given. A man had for many a day sung about

> Davie an' the sky together,

and when asked to explain the rather strange combination he could only say that that was the way he had learned it. The true reading was—

> Davie an' his kye together.

Mistakes are most commonly made with "composed" songs. I once got the following from a person who had written it down from another's singing:—

> Ae bonnie nicht when the heather was bloomin',
> A silent aul' bumbee, a so laden bee.

The second line should have been—

> And the silent hills hummed wi' the sore-laden bee.

Perhaps the responsibility for the transmogrification fell to be shared by both singer and scribe. Sometimes a new reading stumbles into an improvement. The last verse of "Will the Weaver" reads—

> Did ever you see a chimney sweeper
> Half so black as Will the Weaver?
> Hands and face and feet likewise;
> Will went home with two black eyes.

As the poor fellow had been pulled from the chimney, the singer unconsciously made a good emendation when he turned "likewise" into "like swyes." The well-known song, "Woo'd and married and a'," is printed in the books—

> The bride she cam' oot o the byre,
>   And O as she dighted her cheeks,—
> Sirs, I'm to be married the night,
>   And I've neither blankets nor sheets.

A singer once gave us "queets" for "cheeks," and if the former is not the original word it should have been.

Verbal felicities that imply any degree of conscious art or take liberties with the vernacular grammar or idiom are hardly to be looked for in folk-song. At times, however, the folk-songist will in an easy and natural way compass a happy touch.—

> Charlie, O Charlie, come owre frae Pitgair,
> An' I'll gie ye oot a' yer orders;
> For I maun awa' to the high Hielan' hills,
> For awhile to leave the bonnie Buchan borders.

> Wi' him I engagèd a servant to be,
> Which makes me lament I went far frae the sea.

Sometimes an irregularity in the rhythm comes out when sung with fine effect.—

> And the lang weary walks o' Udny (*pron.* Widney)
> Are a' to gang through.

> Bethelnie, O Bethelnie,
> Ye shine where ye stand,
> May the heather bells around you
> Shine o'er Fyvie's land.

> But gin I had the sair hairst shorn,
> An' a' wrocht that I've ta'en in hand,
> I winna bide anither day at Lescraigie,
> Nor yet into Fyvie's land.

Special literary achievements, as we have seen, are not in the folk-songist's line. The old ballad dealt with situations that time and again gave an opening for literary fence which, taken advantage of in a natural way, resulted in strength or pathos. In the more modern ballad there are traces of these qualities of style, the inclination being towards the side of feeling. Humour is as a rule a note of modernity, being comparatively rare in the older forms. Song gets little opportunity for the exhibition of pronounced literary qualities. It deals mostly with the everyday life and feelings of ordinary people. Neither the situations nor the *dramatis personæ* can well be treated as heroic. Anything of this kind would invade and disturb the communal consciousness. Sublimity is of all recognised qualities of style the most alien to this general sense. Pathos is less alien, but even on tendencies in the direction of feeling an early arrest is laid. Humour is the one quality for which there is a natural opening, but not even is humour very pronounced in true folk-song. We have the beginnings of it in pithy phrase and apt characterisation—usually in a satirical vein. It must ever be remembered, however, that to the outside critic these touches may suggest more humour than was intended. Many of them belong to the common stock of rustic epithet, idiom, and phrase.—

> If ye want to learn high farmin'
> Come ye to Beenie's big toon;
> It tak's fourteen pair and some orra
> To work it the hale year roon.

> There's nae chiel here ca'd a foreman
> To earn a muckle big pay;
> The lad that yokes first in the mornin'
> He's foreman for the day.

"Mains" is a greedy farmer and misses no chance of taking a mean advantage.—

> On crafter bodies roon aboot
> He aften gies a ca',
> And buys their bits o' stirkies cheap
> By haudin' on the jaw.

A farm servant thus describes his fare—

> The breid was thick, the brose was thin,
> And the broth they were like bree,
> I chased the barley roon the plate,
> And a' I got was three.

A harvest hand has this complaint against the housekeeper—

> She does all her endeavour
> Her master for to please,
> And when we were leadin' late at night
> She gied us flint for cheese.

> When we tried our teeth to it
> It made us fidge and fyke,
> We had to gang and brak it sma'
> Wi' stanes upo' the dyke.

Wit and humour both mark some of the ribald ditties that may be heard in bothies and farm kitchens; but these songs have been imported and seem to have been the work of the same kind of clever abandoned wags as produced the ditties which have been preserved in the "Merry Muses."

Sometimes in folk-songs the fun is frank and avowed. "The Man to the Green Joe" aims at humour of a topsy-turvy kind, and seems to have some affinity with the nursery rhyme. A verse or two may be given.—

> I rade owre hills and I rade owre happocks,
>   Quo' the man to the joe, quo' the man to the joe ;
> Till I cam' to the kirk that was bigget o' kail castocks,
>   Quo' the merry, merry man to the green joe.
>
> When I gaed to the kirk door, the meal was busy grin'in',
>   Quo' the man, etc.
> When I gaed to the mill door the psalm was busy singin',
>   Quo' the merry, etc.
>
> Oot cam' the maiden, she was the miller's mither,
>   Quo' the man, etc.
> She was riddlin' at her green cheese and siftin' at her butter,
>   Quo' the merry, etc.
>
> Oot cam the miller, they ca'd him Gibbie Reid,
>   Quo' the man, etc.
> Wi' his bonnet on his feet and his breeks on his heid.
>   Quo' the merry, etc.
>
> Owre Benachie I saw a skate flee,
>   Quo' the man, etc.
> And four and twenty little anes fleein' her wi',
>   Quo' the merry, etc.

The most genuinely humorous folk-song that we have is "The Souters' Feast." Its grotesque and rollicking fun recalls Dunbar. The idea may not be original, but the song as we have it is clearly local. It belongs to central Buchan—the Maud district, we should say, judging from evidence of one kind or another ; and it can be traced back for a couple of generations at least, although it does not seem to be old. The vocabulary is in itself a study. The tune to which the song is sung is made up of melodic phrases taken from "Maggie Lauder." We give the refrain only with the first and last verses.—

The Souter's wife she bare a son,
    Tanteerie orum ;
And at the birth there was great fun,
    The eedle and the orum.
The Souters they wid haud a feast,
    Tanteerie orum ;
And wasna that a fine jest ?
    The eedle and the orum
        Thee-a-noddle, thee-a num,
    The eedle and the orum.

Souters cam' frae Auld Deer,
And some o' them was gey and queer;
Souters cam' frae Aiberdeen,
And souters cam' frae yont the meen.

Souters they cam' hine frae Perth,
And souters cam' frae 'neath the earth ;
Souters cam' frae Peterheid,
Wi' fient a teeth in a' their heid.

Souters they cam' doon frae Turra,
And Souters cam' frae Elgin o' Moray ;
* Souters cam' frae Aberdour,
Drivin' in a coach and four.

An ill-faured skyple cam' frae Crimon',
A perfect scunner to the women ;
A muckle hypal haveless loon
Frae the Fite Steen cam' hoiterin' doon.

And when they thocht they a' were come,
A cripple breet cam' owre frae Drum,
Ridin' on a cripple mear,
His apron for his ridin' gear.

As he cam' past the mou' o' hell,
He saw a barkit hide for sale ;
Sae he gaed doon to price the leather,
Tail and lugs and a' thegither.

He gaed doon they kent nae hoo,
But he cam' up wi' a foul mou' ;
Syne a' sat down till their cheer,
It was the lowmons (carcase) o' a mear.

But when wi' feastin' they were fou',
Syne foul mou' began to spew.
First he spewed the rack strap,
And efter that the batter caup.

> Eleven lasts upon a string,
> And efter that an ellisin,
> A bunch o' birse, a ball o' wax,
> And crookit futtles five or sax.
>
> And when they thocht that he was clean,
>   Tanteerie orum,
> He spewed the turkiss and a stane,
>   The eedle and the orum ;
> Syne when they thocht that he was clear,
>   Tanteerie orum,
> Up cam' the steel and a' the gear,
>   The eedle and the orum ;
>   Thee-a-needle, thee-a-num,
>   The eedle and the orum.

Songs are often classified on the basis of subject-matter. This has been done with our ballads, but when we come to ordinary folk-songs the application of the recognised canons does not help us very much. Patriotism, for instance, which is so strong a note in Scottish song in its wide sense, has in the narrower area of folk-song little place and no prominence. The folk-songist is intensely local. It is pretty much his own little district against the world ; for he cannot well rise to wide conceptions of any kind. The stream which flows through his native vale has a geographical name which covers its course from source to sea, but ignoring this the rustic gives to the bit with which he is acquainted a purely local name. His interests and sympathies are all more or less localised, with the result that national sentiment makes no special appeal to him. Setting love songs aside, with which we shall deal presently, we may slump all the rest in one conveniently large and loose class of Songs of Life and Character. Folk-song offers little in the way of generic characterisation or abstract reflection. With it truth, such as it is, has to enter in at lowly doors, and so tends to get embodied in a tale. The incident dealt with usually partakes of the character of an escapade—

> It was a brisk young butcher lad,
>   As I have heard them say,
> He started off from Aberdeen
>   Upon a certain day ;
> And now he says, " My fellows,
>   My fortune I'm to try,
> And I'll awa' to Aikey Fair
>   Some cattle for to buy.

A well-known song of the kind is the " Tarves Rant."—

  Give ear to me ye gay young lads
   That means to tak' a spree,
  I'll tell to you a story
   Withoot ae word o' lee.
  It happened once upon a time
   To Tarves we did go
  To had a spree and hae some fun,
   The truth I'll let ye know.

  To Tarves we for treacle cam',
   We bein' on oor brose,
  Some o' them for boots and shoes,
   And some o' them for clothes;
  There was few there that I kent,
   And as few there kent me,
  But there was ane amo' the lave
   Wha tried to bully me.

  Away to Philip's we did go
   To hae a little fun,
  'Twas there I got ensarèd
   Wi' the maiden o' the inn.
  She was a lovely maiden—
   Gey maiden that she be—
  Twa rosy cheeks, twa rollin' eyes,
   And a lovely maid was she.

Having drunk pretty freely our hero at length sets out for home, but he has not proceeded far when his noisy conduct brings on the scene " a man in blue " who threatens to arrest him. A struggle ensues.—

  He roughly took me by the arm,
   And dragged me to the inn;
  'Twas there we fought right earnestly,
   For it didn't end in fun.

  But surely I'm a profligant,
   A villain to the bone,
  To tear the coat frae aff his back,
   And it nae bein' his ain.
  He tried to shove me in the room,
   His strength he didna spare,
  But I could plainly show him
   That it would tak' a pair.

With assistance the constable gets his man secured as he thinks but the fellow reaches a window and a companion pulls him out.—

> I think you folk in Tarves
> A jail will need to get
> For to lock up your prisoners
> An nae lat them escape;
> For surely it's an awfu' crime
> To brak the Sabbath day
> When searchin' for your prisoners
> When they have run away.
>
> A few mair words I'll tell to you,
> It's nae to my disgrace,
> They brocht me up to Aiberdeen
> To mak' me plead my case;
> But when I heard my sentence,
> I heard it like a shot,
> There was thirty shillin's o' a fine,
> And fifteen for the coat.

Prosaic incidents and occupations sometimes form the theme of the rustic muse.—

> 'Twas in the year auchteen hun'er and aucht
> A road through Buchan was made straught,
> When mony a hielan' lad o' maught
> Cam' owre the Buchan border.
>
> 'Twixt Peterhead and Banff's auld toon
> It twines the knowes and hollows roon,
> Ye scarce can tell its ups frae doon,
> It's levelled in sic order.
>
> The hielan' and the lowlan' chiels
> Cut doon the knowes wi' spads and sheels,
> And bored the stanes wi' jumpin' dreels
> To get the road in order.
>
> There was some in tartan, some in blue,
> Wi' weskits o' a warlike hue,
> And werena they a strappin' crew
> To put the road in order?
>
> And mony a hup and mony a ban
> Got cartin' horse and lazy man,
> For fou and teem and aye they ran
> To push't a bittie forder.

Chiel Chalmers he frae Strichen cam',
Wi' ae black horse as bold's a ram,
Nae ane could match him in the tram,
    He made a braw recorder.

The Meerisons, the Wichts and Giels,
Were swack and willin' workin' chiels,
Sae weel's they banged the barrow steels
    To gar the road gae forder.

The road's as smooth's a harrowed rig,
Wi' stankies on ilk side fu' trig,
And ilk bit burn has noo a brig,
    Where ance we had to ford 'er.

This turnpike it will be a boon
To a' the quintra roon and roon,
And lat folk gae and come frae toon
    Wi' easedom and wi' order.

On fit ye're owre it free to stray,
But if a beast ye chance to hae
At ilka sax miles ye maun pay
    For gaun a bittie forder.

The writer's name gin ye should spier,
I'm Jamie Shirran frae New Deer,
A name weel kent baith far and near,
    I dwell near the road's border.

The various trades that find place in the economy of rural life get due attention at the hands of the folk-songist. It is usually a case of defence or glorification. The miller is a special favourite. Sometimes he speaks for himself. "The Miller of Straloch" has evidently borrowed some ideas from a fellow-craftsman of earlier date.—

I am a miller to my trade,
    I'm miller at Straloch,
I'm a curious cankered carlie,
    My name is Willie Stroth.

I'm engaged with Dr Ramsay,
    He's laird owre all our land,
And when he does give call to me
    I am at his command.

I can play upon the bagpipes
    Wi' muckle mirth and glee,
And I care for nobody, no not I,
    And nobody cares for me.

> The only thing I'm subject to
>   Is a pinch of the broon rappee,
> And when I do fall short o' that
>   I'm no good company.
>
> My mill's got new machinery,
>   She's something strange to me,
> She's of the newest construction
>   My eyes did ever see.
>
> But if I had three roons o' her
>   And a pinch o' the broon rappee,
> I care for nobody, no not I,
>   And nobody cares for me.

Most frequently, however, it is the ploughman that gets premier place at the hands of the folk-songist.—

> The jolly young ploughman lad
>   Goes whistlin' o'er the lea ;
> There's nane in a' the country roon
>   Has a heart sae blythe and free.
> He lo'es his bonnie lassie Jean
>   Sae tenderly and true,
> And Jeanie lo'es the winsome laddie
>   That ca's the cairt and ploo.

Domestic life and relations naturally furnish matter for folk-song. Husband and wife are usually the *dramatis personæ*. The expression of wedded love is hardly to be looked for when we consider how reticent the northern man is when matters of feeling are involved. But evidence of happy relations may appear, for example, in a cordial alliance of husband and wife for the practical ends of making a living or increasing their worldly estate.—

> Quo' Nell my wife the other day,
>   Provisions they are cheap, man,
> And for the trifle it wad tak'
>   A soo we weel may keep, man ;
> Indeed, says I, my thrifty Nell,
> I've jist been thinkin' sae mysel',
> And since we've on the notion fell
>   I'll jist gang doon
>   This afternoon
>   To Matty Broon
>   And very soon
> Bring hame ane in a raip, lass.

The humours of married life provide a congenial theme for the rustic muse. Naturally enough the humour tends at times to become somewhat broad. "The Wee Wifie" illustrates this tendency and would hardly bear *in extenso* quotation.—

    I bocht a wee wifie and feesh her hame,
     My dear, my hussy, my sonsy one;
    But soon my sorrows did begin;
     I'm afraid she'll prove an unthrifty one.
    For she's a' my ain, and she's a' my ain,
     And she's ach, ach, a' my ain;
    Although she be little she's unco dear;
     The wifie and siller she's a' my ain.

Growing sinister at times the rustic muse will fix on domestic infelicities and show the seamy side of life. In such a case it is frequently one or other of the parties concerned that becomes the narrator.—

    I ance had a wife o' my ain,
     Whase heart was as hard's ony timmer,
    To get rid o' the jaud I was fain,
     For she was a d——able limmer.

    To the weans she aften wad cry,
     And my shins wi' a stool she wad rattle;
    But I bein' sic a big size
     She was feart to engage me in battle.

    Ae nicht she cam' hame roarin' fou,
     She gied me a clink wi' the poker;
    I didna ken weel what to do,
     But I hoped the next bumper wad choke her.

    I ordered her oot o' my sicht,
     Or else wi' a raip I wad hang her;
    She gaed to her bed in a fricht,
     And deed the neist mornin' wi' anger.

    Her freens they cam' a' in aboot,
     And ilka ane blintrin' and greetin',
    But for me deil a tear wad come oot,
     For I was richt blithe at the meetin'.

    And noo I've got rid o' my wife,
     Her tongue nae mair on me will bellow;
    I'm resolved for the rest o' my life
     To live as I am a guid fellow.
    Singin', Fal al a riddle a,
     Fal al a riddle adie.

One characteristic feature of our Scottish life in bygone days was the presence and potency of the beggar. The progress of social economics has led to the abolition, in theory at least, of begging; but in former times the Gaberlunzie not only had place and recognition accorded him in the social system, but, as real or supposititious, became the subject of many a ballad and ditty. Some of these, like "The Beggar Man," and "The Beggar's Dawtie," are still widely popular. More recent is "The Begging Trade."—

O' a' the trades that man can try
   The beggin' is the best,
For when a man is wearied
   He can sit down and rest.
      To the beggin' I will go, will go,
      To the beggin' I will go.

Afore that I dae gang awa'
   I'll lat my beard grow lang,
And for my nails I winna pare,
   For beggars wears them lang.

And I will get a meal pock
   Made o' the leather reed,
And it will haud twa firlots
   Wi' room for beef and breid.

Syne I'll gang till a cobbler
   And gar him mak' my sheen
Wi' twa three inches roon aboot,
   A' clouted owre abeen.

And I'll gang till a hatter
   And gar him mak' a hat
Wi' twa three inches roon aboot,
   A' sheenin' owre wi' fat.

At marriage or at market fair,
   Though it be far or near,
I'll mak' a point for to be there,
   For what ye needna speir.

For some will gie me beef and breid,
   And some will gie me cheese,
And roon amo' the marriage folk
   I'll gather bawbees.

> Gin I come on as I wad like
> I will come back and tell ;
> But gin the trade gang——
> I'll keep it tae mysel'.
>   To the beggin' I will go, will go,
>   To the beggin' I will go.

As regards the picture of Scottish social life given in our folk-songs my friend and collaborator, the Rev. Mr Duncan, calls attention to the comparative absence of the convivial element. This discovery has come to us as a bit of a surprise, Burns and his school having done so much to create the impression that the bacchanalian note was an essential feature of the native lyre. Of course, we do find in our folk-songs incidental references to drink and drinking customs, but there is hardly a ditty to be found that charges itself with the task of glorifying these things or even of defending them. Nay, we can see the beginning of a sounder sentiment in reference to intemperance. This is so far explained by the fact that folk song, tending always, as we have pointed out, to bring itself comparatively up to date, has caught somewhat of a modern atmosphere ; but it has equally to be remembered that through all this process of change and replacement, it has clung to its old traditions and ideals ; so that at any point in the history and evolution of folk-song we may expect to find not so much a revision of its attitude towards any cardinal concern of life as a restatement of that attitude in the light of more modern conditions. Hence we conclude that the older folk-songs which the current ones have replaced could not in any large measure have lent themselves to the glorification of "the barley bree," and that, inferentially, our Scottish proletariat have all along been a more sober lot than their critics and censors have been wont to imagine. Pretty certain it is that our bacchanalian ditties are mainly of the "composed" order, and as such are largely imitations—affectations of ideals borrowed from other and warmer climes where an ampler life afforded means and opportunities for conviviality denied to old Scotland in her poverty and isolation. Dealing with current folk-song one has to remark not only the comparative absence of the drinking ditty but the actual presence of the "temperance" lay.—

> Oh, what a mischief whisky's done ;
> Gart mony a man stark naked run,
> Or wi' his nose to ploo the grun
>   When he is gaun hame, O.

It does not so much matter what has been the origin or genesis of these lyrics. The fact remains, significant and satisfactory, that they have been adopted by the folk-songist.—

> O Johnnie, my dear, do ye no think o' risin'?
> The day is far spent and the nicht's comin' on;
> The siller's a' deen, and the gill stoup is empty,
> O rise up, my Johnnie, and come awa' hame.
>
> Wha's that at the door that is speakin' sae canty?
> 'Tis the voice o' my wee wifie, Maggie by name;
> Come in my dear lassie and sit doon beside me,—
> " O rise up, my Johnnie, and come awa' hame.
>
> " The bairnies at hame, they're a' roarin' and greetin',
> Nae meal in the barrel to fill their wee wame;
> While ye sit here drinkin', ye leave us lamentin',—
> O rise up, my Johnnie, and come awa' hame.
>
> " O Johnnie my dear, when we were first acquainted,
> Nae ale house nor tavern e'er ran in oor minds,
> But we spent the lang day 'mang the sweet scented roses,
> And ne'er took a thocht upon gaun awa' hame."
>
> " O weel do I mind on the time that ye speak o',
> These days are awa' and will ne'er come again;
> But as for the present we will try for to mend it;
> Sae gie's yer hand Maggie and I'll come awa' hame."
>
> Then Johnnie got up and he banged the door open,
> Says " Woe to the day to this tavern I came;
> And fare ye weel whisky that mak's me aye tipsy;
> Sae gie's yer hand Maggie and come awa' hame."

The church and religion as such have practically no place in folk-song, which indeed in relation to religion as to love is largely pagan. If ecclesiastical matters are to receive attention at its hands they must as a rule come into the arena of local incident lending itself to satirical comment. The disputed settlement of the Rev. Andrew Cant as minister of the parish of Tyrie gave occasion to an effusion of this kind.—

> Oh wat ye hoo the guise began,
> The guise began, the guise began;
> Oh wat ye hoo the guise began,
> The guise began at Tyrie?
> Lady Tyrie and the laird o' Glack,
> They baith o' them lived in the slack,
> Between the twa there was a pact
> To enter cripple Andrew.

Under the head of Life and Character might be included many of our ploughman ditties, but the Ploughman Song is altogether so characteristic that we should like to give it separate treatment.

We are now left with Love Songs which form, as might be expected, the largest and most interesting class. The folk-songist, it may be premised, is not a perfervid lover. He may feel passion, but he does not care to be too frank in the avowal of it. In the ordinary concerns and relations of life he is rather confident and even at times aggressive, but when he enters the domain of the feelings he begins to be somewhat shy and reticent. Apart indeed from his own individual attitude, passion is too pronounced a mood for the general sense. The communal standards as before come into play and in considerable measure fix for him the conditions of statement and utterance. Again, love in folk-song is largely pagan in character. The joy of life makes frank and fearless appeal to the heart of our young rustic. There may be with him a certain rough-and-ready sense of fairplay and even at times of honour in love's game; but there is hardly a moral sense; conscience rarely makes embarassing or disquieting comment on any situation. This survival of paganism simply betokens the unbroken continuity of folk-song. We have already seen how in manner, in method, and in material, it serves itself heir to the traditions of an undated past, and how it has kept its course along the lower social levels, ever largely beyond the influences that have made or moulded contemporary art and literature. And just as steadily and surely has it ignored any creation or revision of ethical standards that may, at the call of civilisation or religion, have taken place in the higher strata of life. Even in the moral sphere it continues the ancient traditions and remains essentially pagan. A division of love songs into apostrophic and biographic, introspective, or narrative, provides a certain test and measure of their emotional intensity. The apostrophic represents the higher kind of lyric where the lover utters his own feelings in direct appeal to the object of his adoration. It gives unlimited scope for intensity of feeling and expression. As the rustic lover, however, does not want to put things too strongly he is not particularly fond of this direct and personal mode of utterance. He prefers the narrative form as being less compromising. When in a song we encounter real intensity of feeling, avowed and unabashed, we may be pretty sure that we have the work of an individual bard, and something therefore that is not just authentic folk-song.

Passages like

> Ae fond kiss and then we sever,
> Ae farewell, alas! for ever—

would stick in the throat of the genuine folk-songist. The feeling expressed seems to him so exaggerated and unreal that he cannot pretend to identify himself with it. And even though he had some sympathy with the feeling he would hesitate to "give himself away" by so frank an avowal: it would be unmanly. He seeks for a more restrained way of putting things, and so tends to fall back on the narrative form as being more conventional and invading less his native reticence. Nor is he left with only general principles to guide him. Custom and convention have here as elsewhere fixed for him the lines along which he should move. There is the appropriate machinery, the stock of sanctioned situations, the recognised and ready armoury of phrase and epithet. For instance the folk-songist may begin his love lyric by telling you that he walked forth one morning in May. Ladies like to wait till June before venturing abroad on their own initiative. If a river comes into the picture the time is likely to be evening. He takes care to tell you that he was in no hurry but "carelessly did stray." Sure enough he falls in with "a pretty fair maid." "Pretty" is here not an adverb. The maid seems to be there for no other purpose than to be fallen in with. Recognising the dramatic fitness of things the fellow walks up to her and makes overtures right away. The maid does not seek to resent this business-like mode of address. She is quite prepared for it; and things hurry up. The issue is frequently unfortunate; almost always so when the woman is the narrator.

If the folk-songist in general is restrained in his utterance of or allusion to passion, the northern man is specially so. One illustration of this is found in the fact that his stock of love ballads and ditties is largely furnished from the outside. This applies also to "composed" songs. If we examine any representative collection of Scottish songs we shall find that the north has contributed thereto very few love songs and hardly one that can be called passionate. "Tullochgorum" Skinner, the most outstanding song-writer that our county can boast, quite avoided the tender passion in his lyrics. It would be interesting to enquire into the causes of this low erotic temperature; but the speculation would take us too far afield. It is sufficient for our present purpose to state the fact, and to illustrate it in respect of folk-song.

We find then that folk-song circulating in the north, so far as it is indigenous and not imported, shows a lack of fervour when it deals with the subject of love. We have the conventional love-song, which is as usual quite unconvincing.—

> There's toons wi' lasses roon aboot
>   That think themselves fu' braw,
> But there's nae a ane can match my Jean,
>   The lass o' Gonar ha'.
>
> Though ye tak' ne'er sae wide a roon
>   Ye wadna find her peer,
> Though ye should ca' at Tillinamolt,
>   Craigculter or New Deer.
>
> On Cleadie's braes or Skelmanae,
>   Or mossy Middlemeer,
> Even Braco braw she canna shaw
>   A lassie half sae dear.

This is better,—

> 'Twas on a summer's evening
>   As I walked roon the toon,
> I met sweet Marget on a bank,
>   And there we baith sat doon.
> Broomhill's bonnie daughter
>   By all I ever saw,
> Geordie Wilson's bonnie Marget
>   She's stown my heart awa'.

"Boyndlie's Braes" may be taken as a favourable specimen of the local love song, characterised as usual, however, by a certain restraint and a due regard to the practical side of things.—

> Boyndlie's banks and braes are steep,
> And decked wi' flowers o' mony a hue;
> 'Tis there the birdies sing sae sweet,
> And burnies wimple doon the howe.
>   Liltin adie toorin adie,
>   Liltin adie toorin oo.
>
> There does dwell my bonnie Nell,
> Wi' gowden locks and face sae fair;
> And I cam' owre frae Aberdour
> To lat her taste my fruits sae rare.
>
> The lasses a' 'boot Boyndlie braes
> They dress themsel's wi' care and skill,
> But when they a' hae deen their best
> They are but nocht beside my Nell.

Her eyes they shine like diamonds fine,
Her cheeks ye micht bleed wi' a straw,
The blithesome blinks o' Nellie's e'e
Hae fairly stown my heart awa'.

I'm but a prentice laddie yet,
Still workin' for my penny fee ;
But were I laird o' Boyndlie's lands
I wad them a' to Nellie gie.

Oh we are young and hinna wit
O' hoose or haddin to tak' the care ;
But we will wait a fylie yet,
And we will aye be gettin' mair.
  Liltin adie toorin adie
  Liltin adie toorin oo.

The love lay sometimes takes the form of a confidence. In " My Peggie " we have a young fellow discussing his love affair with his mother, who naturally seeks to temper sentiment with worldly wisdom.—

O mither ye maun confess o' a' the girls ye saw
Yestreen at the weddin' sae trig and sae braw,
And wisna my Peggie the flo'er o' them a',
 Like a new blawn rose in the mornin' ?

My Peggie she's fair, my Peggie she's fine,
Her cheeks are like lilies all dipped in wine ;
Her eyes how they sparkle, how brightly they shine
 Like the stars on a fine frosty mornin'.

O Johnnie, O Johnnie, your prospects are sma',
Gin ye mairry Peggie ye'll soon ruin's a' ;
She busks an' she buckles and she gangs aye sae braw,
 But what time does she rise in the mornin'?

O Johnnie, O Johnnie, your prospects are fine,
Your rags and your meal pocks sae finely they shine ;
Mak' ye the vow and the faut will nae be mine,
 But ye'll ruin yersel' and yer mither.

The young man explains that he has had an interview with Peggie's father, with the following result,—

He promised me a pair o' horses and a coo,
Three hundred o' his sheep and twa packs o' guid oo,
To plenish a bit placie at the back o' the broo,
 To be wark tae my Peggie in the mornin'.

> O Johnnie, O Johnnie, ye're far better noo
> When I think o' the dangers o' brakin' a vow ;
> Lat your auld mither's blessing gang wi' Peggie and you,
> An' be wi' ye baith evenin' and mornin'.

We have said that the folk-song lover rather shrinks from making direct appeal to the object of his affections. When he does adopt this mode he is apt to stop short of the abandonment necessary to artistic success at least. A local lover, driven to make appeal, saves the situation a bit by hinting that he is moved by relative as well as personal attractions.—

> I'll let ye know the reason
>   This night how I came here,
> It was to gain the kind favour
>   And the love of you my dear ;
> For lasses like unto you
>   I'm sure they are but few,
> And that's the very reason love,
>   I've fixed my mind on you.
>
> Your yellow hair I do compare
>   To the glittering threads of gold,
> And surely your body has been formed
>   Into some lovely mould ;
> And you've got so much property
>   Few with you can compare ;
> And you're thrice as comely as I've seen ;
>   And you've drawn my heart a snare.

When appeal takes the form of a serenade it is likely to be more compelling. Outside a window on a cold night the rustic lover naturally grows urgent.—

> O Lizzie lass, gin ye'd lat me in,
> I'd enter and crack and nae mak' a din ;
> I wadna wauken ane o' your kin
>   To scauld ye in the mornin'.
>
> I kenna gin't be the snaw and the frost
> Or your neglect kills the most,
> But body and mind I'm tempest-tossed ;
>   I fear I'll dee or mornin'.

The appeal and the plea very often succeed.—

> Rise up, dear love, and open the door,
>   Rise up and lat me in,
> For cauld and frosty is the nicht,
>   And cauld, cauld blaws the win'.

I'll neither rise up nor lat ye in,
   Gae 'wa frae the window pane,
Gang back to them ye was wi' yestreen,
   And be content wi' ane.

Fause, fause was the tongue that tellt ye that,
   For I lo'e nane but yersel',
Rise up, rise up, my ain true love,
   I've a breastfu' o' love to tell.

And how could she doubt the lad she loved?
   Her heart relented soon;
And he clasped in his arms his own true love
   'Neath the light of the silver moon.

That the course of true love does not run smooth is abundantly illustrated in folk-song as elsewhere. In "Jeannie and Jamie" we have the inevitable lovers' quarrel treated in a natural and unaffected way, and ending as usual in a quite happy manner. The song, which is rendered as a duet, was noted down in a Buchan fishing village.—

JEANNIE.—What is the way you're lookin' sae glum,
   And why are ye turnin' awa'?
I'm sure I've deen naething, at least that I ken,
   That's likely to grieve ye ava.

JAMIE.—Yestreen at the ball, ye mind it fu' weel,
   Ye danced wi' nae less than ither three;
And if that's no eneuch noo to grieve me fu' sair,
   For ye ken ye were promised to me.

JEANNIE.—I danced at the ball as a lassie wad dae,
   I ken ye wad ta'en me and a';
But I'll dance wi' a chiel gin I like him fu' weel,
   Ay, and that tae when ye are awa'.

JAMIE.—O little dae ye ken o' the pain at my he'rt;
   Ye're sighin' again to be free;
Ye can gang if ye wish to anither ane's airms,
   But ye ken ye were promised to me.

JEANNIE.—Here is the ring ye gied me afore,
   I'll wear it nae langer ava;
I'll get a lad as guid that'll dae as he's bid,
   Ay, and that tae when ye are awa'.

JAMIE.—Tak' back the ring, Jeannie, tak' it again,
   For oh, it wad grieve me fu' sair;
Ye'll ne'er get a chiel that will lo'e ye sae weel,
   For ye ken ye were promised to me.

JEANNIE.—I'll tak' back the ring, Jamie, tak' it again,
 And together through life we shall fare;
Until death do us pairt ye shall reign in my he'rt;
 And, Jamie, we'll quarrel nae mair.

BOTH.—Noo I am thine, {Jamie, / Jeannie,} noo I am thine,
 And together through life we shall be;
Till death do us pairt ye shall reign in my he'rt,
 For I ken {I am promised to thee. / ye are promised to me.}

"Mormond Braes," for long the most popular of Buchan songs, is the deliverance of a jilted girl. The brave spirit in which she takes her disappointment and the practical sense which marks her outlook illustrate in their own way the moderation and self-restraint which we have claimed as characteristics of northern love. The song will be given in full, words and music, at a later stage.

We have the lament of the girl who, unsuccessful and neglected, concludes that the fates are against her and tries to school herself to bear the inevitable.—

I've won'ert sin' I kent mysel'
 What kept the men folk a' frae me;
For I'm as braw's my cousin Jean,
 And she could get her wile o' three.

I had some thochts o' Donald ance,
 And Donald was my only ane;
Lang, lang I thocht but noo I ken
 The thocht o' Donald's me o'ergane.

He socht a kiss, I gied him twa
 On the craft heid amo' the hay;
Neist time we met he gaped and glowered,
 And turned his heid the other way.

A cloak and sash my auntie sent
 Frae Lunnon Toon for me to wear,
I pat them on and tried my skill
 To catch the lads in Aikey Fair.

But fient a e'e wad blink on me,
 To tell it mak's my heart richt sair;
Sae fare ye weel my cloak and sash,
 I'll never, never wear ye mair,

I've often heard my minnie say,
    (She was the wife that wadna leet),
O the never a lad the lass will get
    But just the ane for her decreet.

Sae I'll gang hame and spin my wheel,
    My saut tear nane shall ever see't;
Lang lang I've thocht but noo I'm sure,
    There's never a ane for me decreet.

More commonly than otherwise love episodes as narrated in folksong have an unfortunate ending. "Allan Maclean," dating from the 18th century, is still a popular song in the north. A few verses may be given.—

Get all things in order,
    I'll write with my pen
The lucks and misfortunes
    Of Allan Maclean.

I was born in the Aulton,
    A minister's son,
Brought up with good learning
    Till my schooling was done.

I went to the College
    A student to be,
But the wedding at Westfield
    It quite ruined me.

George Donald, John Allan,
    Macgregor and I,
We went all to the dancing
    Pretty girlies to spy.

We danced and we drank
    And we took great delight,
Till bonnie Sally Allen
    Came into my sight.

As a rule, however, it is the woman who is represented as the sufferer. "Peggie," or "Lescragie," is a well-known local song embodying an unfortunate incident. It will hardly bear quotation in full, but it contains two or three good verses.—

I'm gaun to yon toonie, Peggie,
    Will I yer bonnie laddie tell?
Will I tell him to send you a letter,
    Or will he come himsel'?

. . . .

> When ye come into the kitchen
> Ye're cheery among us a',
> But when ye gang into the parlour
> Ye'll lat the saut tears fa'.
>
> . . . .
>
> It's my back is sair, Sandy Fraser,
> And sair, sair is my side ;
> And I maun awa' frae Lescraigie,
> For I'm nae langer able to bide.
>
> Gin I had the sair hairst shorn,
> And a' wrocht that I've ta'en in hand,
> I winna bide anither day in Lescraigie,
> Nor yet into Fyvie's land.

Situations of this kind, however, are not always taken so very seriously by the delinquents. We have the roving blade, the frank and unabashed pagan, who braves the thing out and does not much mind though his paganism brings him into collision with church discipline. Like Burns he seems to think himself a bit of a hero and offers to tell you all about his escapade.—

> The parson then began to scold,
> Called me a rovin' blade ;
> And for the deed that ye have done
> Due penance must be paid.
>
> Pay down your guinea and begone,
> And never let me know
> That e'er ye do the like again
> Through a' this life below,—
>
> Through a' this life below again,
> Through a' this life below,
> Whilst ye live upon the bonnie banks
> Of Ugie O.

We have claimed on behalf of our folk-song that as regards the subject of drink its record is cleaner and better than one would have thought. When, however, it deals with love and the relations of the sexes it is, we fear, " no better than it's ca'd." Even in songs that do not mean to be naughty there is often a frankness of statement, a primitive way of putting things, which rather embarrasses the modern editor when he wants to introduce these wildings to good society. Long ago songs were sung in the family circle and in mixed companies that an editor now-a-days would hesitate to print. We must be careful, however, not to confound a standard of taste with an attitude to morality;

and we shall misjudge folk-song if we neglect to apply such an equation as shall get rid of what belongs to time and taste and leave us with the essentials of the problem. But there are ditties whose reception and treatment are not matters of taste. Offending overtly against the general moral sense, knowingly and intentionally bad, they put themselves quite out of court. There is nothing for it but to relegate them to the *index expurgatorius*. The worst kind of ditty, however, circulating among our peasantry is not as a rule home-made. The rustic rhymer may be coarse enough in all conscience, but he lacks the wit and literary equipment to compass the clever obscenity that marks the kind of song that we find, for instance, in the *Merry Muses*. These ribald effusions are evidently the work of men who were as clever as they were abandoned. It is matter of satisfaction that this corrupt element in folk-song is less in evidence than it used to be. The years bring purgation.

The Ploughman Song to which we have already referred merits a special word. It is the most characteristic kind of folk-song which we have, and, as has been said, retains a certain measure of vitality. Its record indeed is not yet closed. The principle has been already laid down that folk-song tends to seek the lowest social level. It follows that, as the farm-servant class represents this ultimate stratum in our rural districts, where alone practically traditional minstrelsy survives, we may expect to find among them the greatest amount of authentic folk-song. They are now in fact pretty much its custodians. As a class our ploughmen have got the hereditary ear and taste for this kind of thing. One observation which we have made has struck us.—Boys belonging to the cottar class will sit dumb during the singing hour in school. Modern songs and even our ordinary Scotch songs do not seem to appeal to them. One might readily conclude that they were hopelessly unmusical. But this is no safe inference. A few years later you may hear these same fellows, now grown to be young men, singing as they sit on the forebreast of their cart, "The Barnyards o' Delgaty," "Drumdelgie," or other ploughman lay, with lusty lungs and in the true native style. Heredity has asserted itself. A remark may be ventured here. As regards the subject of music in the curriculum of our schools we must have been proceeding on wrong lines when in large measure we thus fail to get hold of our bucolic youth, and leave them afterwards to return as best they may to the old native minstrelsy, which alone makes true and compelling appeal to what of aesthetic soul and sense they may possess. We have set aside the foundations which heredity and tradition have laid, and have been trying out of material more or less alien to build a new structure which, having no evolutionary hold of the past, must ever be in weak and parlous case. Instead of seeking to found a national school of music, which alone can make us a musical nation, we have paid foreigners to come over and teach us that we have no music, and to encourage our youth to despise the native minstrelsy and affect a lofty contempt for " the sangs their fathers lo'ed to hear, the sangs their mithers sang."

Ploughman song deals with ploughman life—its occupations and interests. A ploughing match for instance may inspire its rough-and-ready muse.—

   Then some wi' pins and some wi' props
    They a' began a feerin',
   Some o' them seemed to be well pleased,
    And some began a-swearin'.

   Some said their rigs were fearfu' teuch,
    Some said that their's was steenie;
   The furs wad neither cut nor grip,
    Nor yet look square nor bonnie.

   But in spite o' a' difficulties
    They gaily trudged on,
   Aft-times refreshed wi' mountain dew,
    A bannock or a scone.

   The judges trampit ilk man's rig,
    Owre a' its points did grize
   It nearly palled their wits to tell
    Whilk rig for ilka prize.

Harvest is a favourite subject. In days gone by the hairst rig was the scene of some of the happiest experiences of the rural year. Scythers, gatherers, bandsters and rakers, were associated in the work. Besides the regular farm-hands there were others—mostly local tradesmen and cottars' wives, engaged for the season. An eager happy spirit was abroad; everybody was in high good humour. Moving over the field in a body the busy workers had many opportunities for friendly word and merry sally. Acquaintanceships formed on the harvest field often ripened into life-long partnerships. "The Boghead Crew," composed about a generation ago, is a well-known harvest song. It describes, in poor enough rhyme, the harvest hands that worked together one season on the farm of Boghead, in the parish of Pitsligo.—

'Twas in the year eighteen seventy,
  On August the sixteenth day,
From the Parish of Longside
  I northward took my way.

The mornin' bein' fair and clear,
  I travelled on wi' speed,
I was going to be a harvest hand
  On the farm of Boghead.

Now I am not a poet
  Nor yet a learned man,
But I will sing a verse or twa
  And spread them as I can.

John Macnab, oor foremost man,
  Was sturdy, brave, and strang,
Sae canny's he pits in his scythe
  And carries on the thrang.

His gatherer she cam' frae Greenbank,
  Maclennan was her name,
She was the flo'er o' a' oor flock,
  A handsome clever dame.

And Esselmont he ban' to her,
  He was a sturdy chiel,
Ye wadna seen a jollier crew
  Upon a harvest field.

Willie Kidd, oor second man,
  He filled his berth right weel,
He pleasèd baith the girlies,
  The truth I mean to tell.

Jean Forsyth she gathered to him,
  Wi' her lovely curly hair,
I hope they'll meet in wedlock bands,
  They'll be a slashin' pair.

And as for Kidd's bandster,
  They ca' him Geordie Grant,
He's sometimes in a merry mood,
  And sometimes like a saunt.

And so on for some eighteen verses more, making a "stroud" of somewhat formidable dimensions, but yet not too long for the memory and taste of the genuine rustic singer.

    The best as well as the most popular Buchan Harvest Song is "Johnnie Sangster." It has real poetic merit, and, just as this circum-

stance would lead one to expect, can be traced to its author. It was
written by William Scott who was born at Fetterangus in 1785 and
spent his early years in his native district. His experiences as a herd
laddie gave him an insight into rural life which he afterwards turned to
good account, giving in his pastorals and bucolics the most authentic
and convincing pictures of rural life in the north-east which we possess.
The air to which "Johnnie Sangster" is sung is an adaptation of a reel
tune of the same name. A verse or two of the song may be given.—

     O' a' the seasons o' the year
      When we maun work the sairest,
     The harvest is the foremost time,
      And yet it is the rarest.
     We rise as soon as mornin' licht,
      Nae creatures can be blither,
     We buckle on oor finger-steels,
      And follow oot the scyther.

Chorus.—For you Johnnie, you Johnnie,
      You Johnnie Sangster,
     I'll trim the gavel o' my sheaf,
      For ye're my gallant bandster.

     A mornin' piece to line oor cheek
      Afore that we gae forder,
     Wi' clouds o' blue tobacco reek
      We then set oot in order.
     The sheaves are risin' fast and thick,
      And Johnnie he maun bind them,
     The busy group for fear they stick
      Can scarcely look behind them.

     I'll gie ye bands that winna slip,
      I'll plait them weel and thraw them,
     I'm sure they winna tine the grip,
      Hooever weel ye draw them.
     I'll lay my leg oot owre the sheaf,
      And draw the band sae handy,
     Wi' ilka strae as straught's a rash,
      And that will be the dandy.

  The ploughman song, however, most commonly resolves itself into
a narrative of the singer's experiences at some farm where he has been
fee'd. He characterises the place, the farmer, his fellow-servants, male
and female, the horses, the work, the food—often in caustic vein and
with occasional touches of genuine humour. These effusions are formed
on a pattern and draw as usual on a common stock of phrase and

epithet; while they not infrequently get adapted to a place other than the original one by a change of name. Many of these ditties are rustic satires. A farmer who by tyrannical or niggardly conduct gains a bad reputation among farm-servants may be made the subject of a song in which his faults are held up to ridicule or reprobation. The invective is not of a polished order. The ploughman always speaks his mind in quite a direct way. We give some verses from a local song called "Swaggers" to illustrate the kind of effusion to which we refer.—

> Come all ye jolly ploughman lads
>   That whistles through the fair,
> Beware o' gaun to Swaggers,
>   He'll be in Porter Fair.
> He'll be aye lauch, lauchin',
>   It's he'll be lauchin' there,
> And he'll hae on the blithest face
>   In a' Porter Fair.
>
> He'll tell ye a fine story,
>   Sae little's ye'll hae adee ;
> And aye he'll call the ither gill—
>   Get them for little fee ;
> And aye he'll call the ither gill
>   Until he get ye fou,
> And gin ye gang to Swaggers
>   Sae seen's he'll gar ye rue.
>
> He'll tell ye o' some plooin' match
>   That isna far awa',
> And gin ye clean your harness weel
>   Ye're sure to beat them a' :
> For it has gained the prize before
>   At ilka country show,
> And gin that ye lat it fa' back
>   Ye'll be thocht little o'.
>
> It's a pair o' blues that leads the van,
>   Sae nimbly as they go ;
> A pair o' broons that follows them
>   Wha never yet said no.
> A wee bit shaltie ca's the neeps,
>   And oh it is but sma',
> But Swaggers he will gar ye trew
>   It's stronger than them a'.
>
> It's Swaggers in the harvest time
>   He's got too much to do,
> A twa three jovial laddies
>   That ca's the cairt and ploo ;

But he'll gang on some twenty miles
  Where people disna him ken,
And there he'll fee his harvest hands
  And bring them far frae hame.

He says unto the foreman,
  Keep aye the steady grin,
And dinna lat the orra lads
  Stan' idle at the en';
For I pay ye a' good wages,
  And so ye must get on,
And gin ye binna able,
  There's another when ye're done.

Now the harvest's ended
  And the fee into our pouch,
Sae merrily as we'll tramp the road,
  We're oot o' the tyrant's clutch;
Sae merrily as we'll tramp the road,
  For we've gotten oor freedom noo;
And we'll gang nae mair to Swaggers,
  Sae sair's he gars ye rue.

We shall have occasion at a later stage to submit one or two of our ploughman songs in full, words and music. Meantime we give one complete as far as words are concerned which may be taken as a good and typical specimen of this the most characteristic kind of folk-song which we have.—

I gaed up to Alford for to get a fee,
I fell in wi' Jamie Broon and wi' him I did agree.
  Chorus.—Tum a hi dum do, tum a hi do day.

I engaged wi' Jamie Broon in the year o' ninety-one
To gang hame and ca' his second pair and be his orra man.

When I gaed hame to Gyes o' Tough, 'twas on an evening clear,
And oot aboot some orra hoose the gaffer did appear.

I'm the maister o' this place, and that's the mistress there;
And ye'll get plenty cheese and breid, and plenty mair to spare.

I sat and ate at cheese and breid, till they did roon me stare,
And fegs I thocht that it was time to gang doon and see my pair.

I gaed to the stable my pairie for to view,
And fegs they were a dandy pair, a chestnut and a blue.

On the followin' mornin' I gaed to the ploo,
But lang lang or lowsin' time my pairie gart me rue.

My ploo she wisna workin' weel, she widna throw the fur,
The gaffer says, There's a better ane at the smiddy to gang for.

When I got hame the new ploo she pleased me unco weel,
But I thocht she wad be better gin she had a cuttin' wheel.

I wrocht awa' a month or twa wi' unco little clatter,
Till I played up some nesty tricks and broke the tattie chapper.

The gaffer he got word o' this and orders did lay doon,
That if I did the like again he wad pit me frae the toon.

We hae a gallant bailie, and Wallace is his name,
And he can fair redd up the kye when he tak's doon the kaim.

We hae a little bailie and Jamieson's his name,
And he's gane doon to Alford and raised an awfu' fame.

He's gane doon to Charlie Watt for to get a dram,
But lang, lang or I won doon the laddie couldna stan'.

We hae a gallant kitchie lass, and Simpson is her name,
And for to tell her pedigree I really wad think shame.

She dresses up on Sunday wi' her heid abeen the level,
Wi' twa raw o' ivory wad scare the verra devil.

Noo my song is ended, and I won't sing any more,
And if ony o' ye be offended ye can walk outside the door.
  Tum a hi dum do, tum a hi do day.

If love appears in these Ploughman Songs it represents little more than the natural and inevitable association of Jock and Meg as lad and lass for the time being. There is in it neither idealism nor chivalry. The roving life which the farm servant class lead colours their love affairs and gives them a complexion all their own. Thrown together for six months or a year the ploughman and the servant girl adopt each other *pro tem.* and without prejudice. People in the better ranks of life are tempted to call this a liason; but it is hardly fair to use terminology borrowed from a social sphere where conditions are different. Its application is bound to misinterpret the situation to some extent. In any case the parties pay little or no heed to the views of what is to them an outer world. Social Ishmaelites throughout the generations our farm servants have no public opinion to reckon with, but are a law unto themselves. They have the courage of their practices, and never seem ashamed even when the results of their amours come to light individually, or afterwards in the mass form matter of sinister statistical statement and comment. We are not, however, dealing with the moral aspects of the question. We simply have to recognise that sexual relations in this particular stratum of life are about as nearly natural as the law will allow them to be, and that sexual love appears in their songs pretty much as it would have done in pagan times. But it should in justice be added that however free the relations of young men and women may be about our farms, these persons when once married exhibit as a rule a degree of conjugal fidelity that compares favourably with that found in the higher grades of society. The gross element in our ploughman ditties may readily enough escape the collector. The words sung or said to him may appear free from objection; but likely enough the version is unoffending because incomplete, the excised stanzas being kept for special occasions and company. And, inasmuch as the whole song is a kind of patchwork, the absence of any particular bit creates no organic hiatus that might lead the collector to suspect the existence of an esoteric version.

We come now to the music of our folk-songs. It is more individual and characteristic as well as much older than the words; and yet it has received ever so much less attention. This tendency to ignore the tunes and concentrate attention on the words has largely ended in a divorce of the two elements that constitute a song properly so-called. And both have suffered. Taken apart from the music the words have come to be judged mainly by literary standards. But "good is good for what it suits"; and the words of a song being intended for singing cannot fairly be judged apart from the music. Some lyrics read well and yet do not or would not sing well; while verses may be quite effective when sung and yet appear to have no particular merit when looked on simply as literature. We have already referred to the way in which our old ballads have been treated. The literary quality of these compositions is such that they challenge attention on their own account, tempting people to collect and print them without their tunes, until instead of ballads we have now got ballad poetry. This is a kind of misrepresentation against which one would protest, although there is little hope now that things will ever be put right; the objectionable practice has gone on too long, and the attitude engendered by it has got too deeply confirmed. Much worse has been the mischief wrought in the domain of song by this way of looking at things. The poetry of our ballads has been saved if the tunes have mostly gone; but our folk-songs, both words and music, have in the mass been quite overlooked. When the words were the main thing with collectors, and these had little or no literary distinction, the whole song went by the board. When, however, these compositions are taken as complete products—words and music, and judged by the effect they produce when sung, many of them merit attention and would well justify collection; while many more, although poor enough, have a message and a significance in reference to popular minstrelsy which should prevent them from being altogether overlooked. But if either of the two component parts of folk-song is to be looked at apart from the other it is the tune that deserves this separate attention. Yet so far have collectors been from recognising this that, when the quality of the words of a folk-song dictated its rejection, the tune was not allowed to make any appeal against the decision, although in very many cases its high melodic merit might well have established a claim that it be preserved on its own account.

This is the most regrettable result that has followed from collectors approaching the subject of folk-song from a wrong stand-point. Such attention as folk-melody has hitherto received has too often involved misrepresentation. A good deal of our recognised Scottish melody is founded on folk-tune, but the great bulk of it has been edited, in some cases almost out of recognition and identification. It was during the 18th century that Scottish melody got consolidated. Editors and compilers thought it incumbent on them to pay deference to the prevailing taste, and aimed at bringing the old tunes as far as possible into line therewith. Indeed one cannot well trust any version of an old air given by those editors unless it is confirmed—which it seldom is—by what we still find floating about traditionally. Even when collectors would give specimens of the old traditional airs sung to ballads or songs there is an evident inclination to apologise for the wildings. The attitude is a risky one. It brings with it a temptation to tone down the peculiarities which, while they are thought to offend, are the very things that give the airs in question character and distinction. On the other hand when editors give specimens of the old tunes as more or less curiosities, one has considerable confidence in the genuineness of what they give.

Motherwell in his *Minstrelsy Ancient and Modern* (1827), gives an appendix of traditional ballad airs numbering 33. The prefatory note shows his attitude. He says that the music which he prints has been obtained at great cost and that considerable pains have been taken to note it down with fidelity and accuracy. " Whatever the musician may think of its worth the antiquarian, it is believed, will not lightly pass it by, but on the contrary rejoice with an exceeding gladness that some little has been done to transmit it purely and undefiled to posterity.' Kinloch's *Ancient Scottish Ballads*, published in the same year as Motherwell's work, has a similar appendix of tunes numbering 17. Whether they be strictly conform to musical principles he thinks it needless to inquire. They are given, he says, exactly as they have been in use to be sung to their respective ballads and are reduced into such time as best suited the manner of singing them. "As they in general possess that simplicity peculiar to ancient airs they seem upon the whole to be worthy of preservation." All this is in various ways instructive. For one thing it seems strange that so much should be made of collecting a few traditional tunes in days when they must have been as thick as blaeberries. Even to-day when these folk-tunes are dying out a local collector would very soon have a bigger budget than Motherwell's and Kinloch's put together. In Professor Child's monumental work there is given a set of unpublished ballad airs amounting to between 50 and 60. A few are from a MS. about 1783, but these have been noted by a man of defective musicianship. A number are from a MS. about 1830, and appear as a rule to be fairly reliable. A few of the airs are from a MS. by C. K. Sharpe. The rest are from recent tradition. Dean Christie is the one man who has hitherto succeeded in making a collection of folk-tunes extensive enough to provide materials for studying the product; but he has himself largely failed to use aright his great opportunity, while at the same time he has prevented his successors from using his materials by editing them out of reliability. Altogether it may be said that only since the recent folk-song revival sent workers into the field to collect at first-hand and to record their finds with scrupulous accuracy and fidelity have we got any considerable body of traditional melodies that can be taken as genuine and trustworthy specimens of folk-tune. "Book" tunes, so far from guiding us, fall themselves to be tested by these recent finds; and not many of them come through the ordeal quite satisfactorily. We are indeed only now beginning to see how our popular minstrelsy has been doctored by collectors and editors. Although very much remains to be done, our own quest even within the bounds of Buchan has already resulted in the accumulation of several hundreds of first-hand records of folk-tunes and their variants; so that we may claim to have a quantity of material large enough to justify us in attempting a little generalisation in a cautious and tentative way.

To understand folk-song we must have a lively and constant apprehension of the fact that, like the speech of the child or the pure illiterate, its acquisition is a matter of imitation, and its retention a matter of memory. This applies to the words generally, and to the music always. It is the key of the situation, and must be firmly held and constantly applied. For people who always conceive of language as represented in print, and of music as represented in notation, it is most difficult to realise the standpoint from which the folk-song man regards the words and especially the tunes of his ditties. In fact, it can only be done approximately; but only in so far as we succeed in identifying ourselves with this peculiar attitude of the singer to his songs can we hope to understand folk-song and its tantalising problems.

What then are some of the main characteristics of folk-tune as we find it still lingering in our north-eastern angle? To begin with, we may say that it is economic of melodic material, and simple in structure. Keeping in view the special conditions of folk-song just referred to, we shall admit that this is quite natural and to be expected. The rustic singer has to pick up his tunes by ear, and carry them in his memory without even a mental picture of their notational representation. Further, his music is mainly an instrument of utterance. The words are with him the first and chief consideration. The tune is just a fine way of delivering them, and bears somewhat of the same relation to them as a short and simple chant does to a long prose psalm. Folk-tunes consist, originally at least, of only one strain. Second strains may be looked on as excrescences. They are an afterthought and come with musical development. They seem to have had an instrumental origin, and to aim at exploiting the resources of an extended scale. That the second strains involve an extension of the range of the melodies can be shown statistically. The unit of the tempered scale is the semitone, and there are 12 of these in an octave. The range of a tune, or the interval between its lowest and highest notes, may thus be conveniently expressed in terms of semitones. Johnson's *Musical Museum*, the most important of our older collections of Scottish Song, contains some 600 airs, the average range of which is a little over 17 semitones. As a representative modern collection we may take the Balmoral edition of Wood's "Songs of Scotland." Here, mainly through the rejection of the airs of extravagant range given in Johnson, the average has fallen to a little over 16. The tunes in these collections have as a rule two strains. Christie, who has brought his folk-tunes in line with the "book" songs by finding or faking second strains, almost rivals Johnson with an average range for his airs of nearly 17 semitones. Motherwell and Kinloch, practically innocent of second strains, work out at from 13 to 14. Their collections are small and represent chiefly the simpler ballad airs. But we have taken from our own collection of folk-tunes a number about equal to that in Christie's book, and find the average range to be about 14½ semitones. And the one difference between Christie's collection and ours is that while second strains are with him the rule they are with us the exception. These figures are instructive. The ill-advised attempt to expand our old traditional melodies or to replace them by extended tunes in the conventional manner has in many cases quite killed the songs. Take "The Gaberlunzie Man" for example. In the *Museum* it is set to a tune which, besides covering nearly two octaves, is cranky and would never fix itself in the mind of any ordinary singer. The result is that as a book song it is dead. I never heard anybody even attempt to sing it from the book. But the ballad, as set and sung to a crisp and vigorous folk-tune of one strain, is alive to-day among our rustic singers. I have already noted it some eight times in our neighbourhood.

Not only are folk-tunes economic of material, but their structure is simple. A tune extends as a rule to four lines, with at times the addition of a short refrain of meaningless syllables. Sometimes there are four distinct lines of melody; sometimes there are three; and sometimes only two—with varying schemes of repetition and arrangement. The most characteristic arrangement of the binomial makes the third line a repetition of the second, and the fourth a repetition of the first, like the rhyme-scheme of the *In Memoriam* stanza, which may be represented by the formula *abba*. The last line, however, is often treated with considerable freedom. This peculiar form is said to be Celtic. Its purpose strikes us as being mnemonic. It must further be allowed that, in securing variety and avoiding monotony when the tune comes to be often repeated, the arrangement in question makes the most of the slender material, as may be seen by comparing it with the more modern scheme *abab*.

There is a distinction as to rhythm between two classes of folk-tunes, and this, corresponding in a general way with the classification of the words into ballads and songs already given, emphasises our point as to their respective origins. The airs to which our old ballads are sung are mostly in three-pulse time, but so treated in respect both of tempo and rhythm as to give the feeling of freedom and even irregularity.

These tunes we think had originally been a kind of chant or recitative—
pretty much *ad libitum* as regards time and accent. When musicians
came to express them in notation they chose $\frac{3}{4}$-time as fitted to represent
approximately the peculiar rhythm of these primitive melodies. But one
must hear them rendered in the traditional manner by some authentic
exponent to appreciate their true character as to rhythm and accent.
Certain notes in the tune become as it were rallying points whereon the
singer hangs beyond the allotted time as if loth to leave them. The
note *me* is a favourite one for this "fond delay." Martial ballads tend
to appear in some form of common time—just as we should expect,
having affinities with "the tramp of armed men." Songs as distinct from
ballads are usually sung to airs in common time. This is also what we
should expect, if, as we have contended, song originated in connection
with the dance, the primitive rhythms of which were in common time.

Into the details of melodic form we cannot enter with any degree of
fulness. It would involve too much that is merely technical. Some
brief notes, however, may be given. Our old traditional melodies are
marked by certain peculiarities. Modern melody has its form and
features largely conditioned by the interests of harmony, the development
of which has led among other things to a certain recasting of the scale.
Our folk-tunes arose before the days of harmony, and have been evolved
independently of it. Many of them are in the ancient modes. These
modes as we know them belong to the early centuries of the Christian
era, but their historical origin is Hellenic. Modern music recognises
only two modes, the major and the minor; but in ancient times there
were as many modes as there were degrees in the ordinary diatonic scale.
The modal tunes, as we call them, have no keynote in the modern sense
of the term, and convey no feeling of tonality as we interpret it. They
may be founded as we have said on any note of the diatonic scale, the
intervals of which undergo no alteration or relative adjustment. The
modes most frequently used in ancient Scottish melody are the Dorian,
founded on D; the Mixolydian on G; and the Aeolian on A; or in
Sol-fa nomenclature, which is less liable to be misunderstood, the *Ray* mode,
the *Soh* mode, and the *Lah* mode. The final note of the tune guides us
in determining the mode. Thus a tune ending in *ray* is a Dorian, while
one ending in *soh* is a Mixolydian. The Dorians are the most numerous
and the most characteristic. Aeolians are also common. Their mode is
just our minor scale without the accidentals. The absence of the sharp
seventh in a cadence resolving upwards gives them a fine old-world

flavour. The Mixolydians, less numerous than the other two classes, are often distinguished by a certain stately beauty. It is a common practice to note the Dorian as a minor with the 6th sharpened, and the Mixolydian as a major with the 7th flattened. This we think a mistake. Musicians may understand it, but to most people it suggests that these modal tunes take systematic liberties with the scale. This misrepresents them. The deference thus paid to modern feeling may be well meant, but we should frankly face the situation, recognise the peculiar character of these tunes, and educate ourselves to feel and appreciate it. The ear trained on modern modes needs such an education. The natural impression when one first hears a modal tune is that there is something wrong or at least incomplete about it. Yet the rustic, inheriting the traditional ear for these things, sings his modal tunes with perfect confidence and the utmost relish. All which is a kind of revelation to the collector when he first takes the field.

Our earliest folk-tunes that appear in the major mode employ a form of the scale which we call Pentatonic, inasmuch as it is limited to five notes, the 4th and 7th (*fa* and *te*) being omitted. The origin of this scale has given rise to any amount of discussion, and quite a number of theories have been advanced to account for it. For those people who do not hanker after recondite explanations it may be enough to regard the pentatonic scale simply as selective. The old singer wanted bold intervals, and, feeling uncomfortable with anything less than a whole tone, avoided the 4th and 7th of the scale which were likely to land him in moves of a semitone. The more modern vocalist, getting his ear trained by instrumentation, has no objection to semitones, so he fills up his scale, and, when an old pentatonic melody passes through his hands, he is apt to introduce the missing degrees of the scale as passing notes. In this way a good few of our old pentatonic airs have got their original character overlaid.

A feature of folk-tune, to which incidental reference has just been made, is the boldness of the intervals—the fondness for a kind of "gapped" scale. This can be felt in a general way. It is of course pretty much a relative matter as beween folk-tunes and other tunes, and for its due appraisement and precise statement a good deal of statistical work would fall to be done. What we have ourselves done in this direction rather inclines us to think that there is a danger of overdoing the "gap" theory.

Transitions are unknown in old traditional airs. Devices too of imitation, symmetrical balancing of phrases, and modulation in general, are hardly to be found in anything beyond the germ stage. Chromatic notes are never used. The appearance of accidentals—except at times in case of the flat seventh, is due to the notation employed. The sharp seventh in the minor always betrays the touch of a later hand.

The origin of our folk-melody cannot in the nature of things be traced. To such things indeed there can be no definite beginning. If we select a point in the early history of our people we may suppose a body of melody in existence at that time which, in relation to the music of after centuries, may be considered archetypal. A process of evolution would ensue. We should have the recognised factors of such a process all in operation more or less—heredity, environment, natural selection, and the survival of the fittest. Special circumstances in the history of a people have to be taken into account. For one thing it would seem that our lowland ancestors must, along with place-names, have taken over a very considerable body of melody from the Celts whom they displaced. We have referred to the Celtic form of the melodic quatrain represented by the formula *abba*. Of tunes constructed on this principle we have already noted in our district between 40 and 50, a larger proportion indeed than we have found in collections of airs professedly Gaelic. So large an element in our lowland folk-tune cannot well be explained as adventitious or intrusive in an occasional way, but seems to argue derivation of some kind. This conclusion is strengthened by an examination of the cadences of our folk-tunes. These are largely founded on Gaelic models. The common Gaelic cadence is trochaic, and this our Scottish song has imitated as far as the genius of the language will well permit, and even beyond that point. The tune in such a case ends on an accented note, which sometimes, through the prolongation of the penultimate, may receive a secondary accent. Frequently this final place is filled by an "O." Along with music we have mentioned place-names as part of our inheritance from the ancient inhabitants of our land, and it is according to the fitness of things that these names should be so often worked in at the end of a line of a Scotch song as lending themselves *con amore* to the demands of an old Gaelic cadence. To these evidences of a Gaelic derivation for much of our lowland folk-melody, large and obvious, fall to be added some other evidences which, though not quite so obvious, point to the same conclusion. Into these, however, we have no time to enter.

In its course down the centuries folk-tune has got reinforced at various points and from various sources. Besides the large body of Gaelic melody which it took over long ago, it has from time to time borrowed individual tunes from the Highlander. Irish tunes too have found their way into our area. These, we think, had as a rule been brought home by soldiers who had picked them up from the singing of Hibernian comrades around the camp fire during the Napoleonic wars. English and book tunes too have got annexed from time to time. Song, associated at its start with the dance, has time and again renewed the intimacy to the extent of borrowing tunes, chiefly reels and strathspeys. These have mostly been picked from the violin, but the bagpipe too has been laid under contribution. After all, however, the mass of our folk-melody is original, and has its main roots back of all these accessions and reinforcements.

The peculiar circumstances attending the life and transmission of folk-music has given it a character which differentiates it widely from " composed " music. While the latter remains practically fixed in form, the former may and does get varied to almost any extent as it passes from mouth to mouth down the generations. Each singer is likely to alter something, to give at least some turn of his own to a note or phrase —unconsciously if not of set purpose. There is no standard of appeal as in the case of book music. Every man's way is right in his own eyes. Hence arise those endless variants which are apt to become the despair of the conscientious collector. He cannot take one version and say he has got the tune, so long as there are other versions in vogue. He must take all he can get. But then where is the tune? What is it? He finds he must revise his definitions. A folk-tune is certainly no individual entity. It is hardly even a generic conception. After much comparative study of his brood of variants he may think he has discovered something common to them all. He can trace a framework on which they are all built. It is a skeleton affair at best, rickety and evasive, but it is something and he is thankful for it—thankful until he comes across another variant which knocks a plank out of his poor structure ; and then another which knocks away another plank until—well, he is prepared for anything. In despair he falls back on a kind of intuition, through the exercise of which he feels that his ruck of records are all variants of *something* which is at once the air and in it. This is of course an extreme case, but with this characteristic fluidity of folk-tune, as it has been called, the collector has ever to reckon. For the practical purpose of publication he may choose a version—or make one ; but when he aims at dealing with the subject scientifically he must have regard to all the variants in each case. He will find that they are not hap-hazard or wanton. There is some method in their apparent madness—principles underlying this bewildering flux. These the student must try to grasp and appraise. For one thing variational range may in a general way be taken as a measure of age.

There is the variation which represents the idiosyncracy of some individual singer. To qualify this we should, where possible, apply the personal equation. Further, it is worth while tracing the pedigree of versions where this can be done. Then there is the communal trend within a given area. Doubtless there is something in what an eminent folk-song authority says—that it will probably be found that each county so varies the scheme of a tune that in time it develops racial traits, just as the county has developed racial traits in the music of speech. It has to be remembered, however, that the phonic differences of speech in contiguous counties are comparatively slight, and often subtly elusive. Differences in the scheme of a tune must in the nature of things be overt. When there is anything distinctive in the folk-tune of a particular area the main explanation will we think be found in the selective instinct of the people, certain kinds of melody being for one reason or another grateful to particular communities. Thus tunes of the " Pitgair " type appear to be favourites in our north-east angle. In the mass folk-tune must ever and necessarily represent the communal musical sense, and be the embodiment of its ideals.

We have dealt with the words and the music of folk-song, giving each branch some separate treatment. We propose now to give some specimens of the folk-song as a complete product—verses and tune together. This combination alone makes a song. We have already protested against the practice of divorcing these two component parts. Ballads and songs were made to be sung, and are always so rendered by the people whose heritage they are. One would imagine from the way some editors deal with the subject that ballads in particular were made for reciting, and were usually so rendered by the people. So far from this being the case, it is difficult to get these things recited by the folk-song man. Over and over again he will stick and have to take again to singing to recall his words. Even as regards the words it may be taken that a ballad got from recitation is got at second-hand.

A lyric may be found sung to more than one tune, and on the other hand the same tune may do duty for different lyrics. Both things are quite common. The mating of words and music is a task which any good folk-songist will undertake without much hesitation. What we have said on the subject of variation must be borne in mind. We get different versions of the words of any particular ballad or song, and we get different versions of the tune; but the variational range is much wider in the case of the music than it is in the case of the verses. A little study of the matter prepares us for this. Again, we may collate the different versions of the words of a ballad or song that are in circulation, and from the lot construct what we think a better version than either of them. This is somewhat risky, although when a practical purpose is in view it may be considered allowable. To apply the eclectic method to the variants of a tune is a kind of outrage, but we fear it has often been done in past days. An editor may use his discretion at a time and in regard to some detail. But all changes are more or less dangerous. An editor may claim that he is as much entitled to modify a tune as is the rustic singer from whom he notes it down—and more so, in virtue of his own superior musical knowledge. But paradoxical as it may appear to some people, the rustic's ignorance is his safety, while the light on which the other relies may only lead astray. The former can only change in terms of folk-tune; the latter may change in terms of Handel, Wagner, Lowell Mason, or himself. For ordinary publication one version of the tune must be selected and adhered to. In the work of selection the editor will be guided by various considerations. For people who have never come into direct contact with folk-tune it may be as well to mention that the authentic rendering is traditional, and can be only approximately represented in musical notation. For the purpose of catching and preserving this traditional style phonograph records might with advantage be employed. Folk-songs are sung at a somewhat slow rate. As to pitch, each singer has his own. We have noted our tunes in keys to suit average voices.

The following ten songs which we give as concrete illustrations—words and music—of the subject of our paper, represent but a very small fraction af the material available. They are all known and sung more or less in Buchan at the present time, having been noted down from the lips of local singers quite recently, some of them a number of times. Besides being sung in our district they have some special connection with it. This of course comes mainly from the side of the words. As we have seen, the true folk-tune cannot be assigned to any definite locality, although its vogue may be greater in one than in another, and may even have come to be limited to some particular one.

We give first a local specimen of the ballad with tune in ¾-time.

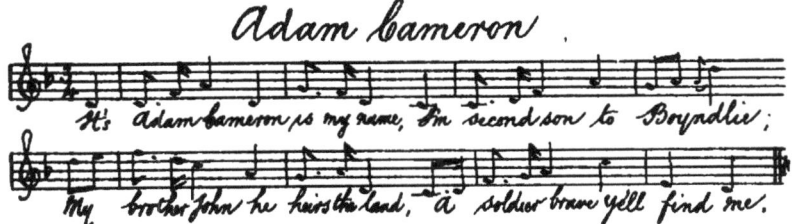

It's Adam Cameron is my name,
  I'm second son to Boyndlie;
My brother John he heirs the land,
  A soldier brave ye'll find me.

When parting with my bonnie love,
  Her hand in mind was lockèd,
And for to drive dull care away
  I spoke as if I jokèd.

She said "Farewell now, you must go,
  Though you say I'm your charmer;
My parents say, 'Your heart now keep,
  And give it to a farmer.'"

Then stately I did step away
  To go on to Dumbarton,
And I had on my highland dress
  As lieutenant to the captain.

Soon after this a letter came
  From Fanny as a token,
To show me and to let me know
  They wished her vows were broken.

When reading it her brother came
  And asked me for a furlough
To go and see his sister wed,
  He wished to go to-morrow.

I said, "You must get here a coach
For me and Chaplain Findlay,
And you will go along with us
To the bonnie Parks of Boyndlie."

At Boyndlie's Parks we Fanny saw,
I said, "Are you wed, Fanny?"
"Oh no," she said, "they wish me wed
To a farmer, if I wed any."

I laid my broad sword on her knee,
We kissed and shook hands over;
Then Chaplain Findlay made us one,
I'm husband now and lover.

The ballad is given by Dean Christie, whose version of the words we follow, curtailing them a bit, however, as they are not particularly interesting. Mr John Milne reads "Duncan" for "Adam." We have noted the tune as a minor. It can be read as a Dorian by throwing off the flat in the signature which has got no work to do. Christie gives a different air, with as usual two strains.

"The Battle of Harlaw" exemplifies the martial ballad sung to a vigorous tune in common time with a refrain. The ballad is too long for reproduction here, and besides it is already in print and fairly well known. We give the tune with one verse (not the first) and the refrain.—

Oh cam' ye frae the Highlands, man,
Or cam' ye a' the wye?
Or did ye see Macdonald's men
Come frae the Isle o' Skye?

Wi' a dadium a derry-dee,
A dadium a die.

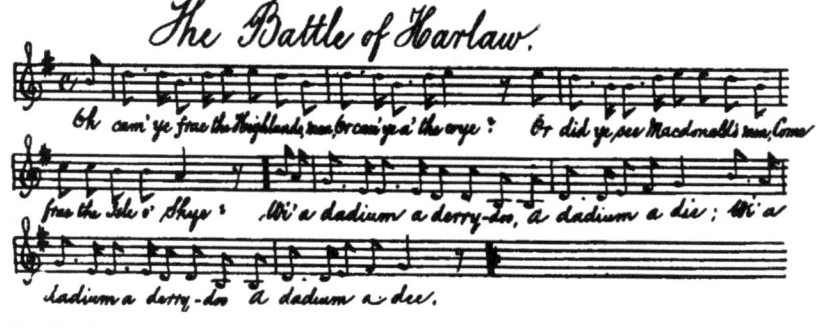

The version of the tune here given has been communicated by Mr W. Forbes, Newark, Ellon. I have got another version from Mr James Knox, Peterhead, who caught it from the singing of a beggar woman; and I have noted another from a local singer. In Child there is given a version got in the Garioch by Mr W. Walker, Aberdeen. It is noted in 6-8th rhythm, but this is a detail which the musician can discount. These four sets of the air are all pretty much alike. Mr Walker's version is pentatonic, and this is presumably the oldest form. Mr Forbes thinks that the air is the original from which Nath. Gow worked up his "Miller o' Drone," the order of the strains being reversed. Rev. Mr Duncan has noted a version which, both in notes and in the order of the strains, is just Gow's "Miller." The refrain as I have heard it rendered is sung with a strong bagpipe grind.

We will now give one or two specimens of the local love song.—

As I gaed doon by Strichen toon
   I heard a fair maid mournin',
And she was makin' sair complaint
   For her true love ne'er returnin'.
It's Mormond Braes where heather grows,
   Where afttimes I've been cheery,
It's Mormond Braes where heather grows,
   And there I've lost my dearie.

Ref.—Sae fare ye weel, ye Mormond Braes,
   Where aften I've been cheery,
Fare ye weel, ye Mormond Braes,
   For it's there I lost my dearie.

Oh I'll put on my goon o' green,
   It's a forsaken token,
And that will lat the young men know
   That the bands o' love are broken.

There's mony a horse has snappert and fa'en,
   And risen and gane fu' rarely,
There's mony a lass has lost her lad,
   And gotten anither richt early.

There's as guid fish into the sea
   As ever yet was taken,
I'll cast my line and try again,
   I'm only ance forsaken.
Sae I'll gae doon to Strichen toon
   Where I was bred and born,
And there I'll get anither true love
   Will mairry me the morn.

"Mormond Braes" is usually attributed to Dr Gavin of Strichen, father of the late Dr Gavin. It has, however, shared the fate of other contributions to the folk-lyre by being subjected to changes and addenda. Mr John Milne can give an account of some of these changes and interpolations, with the names of the singers who introduced them and approximate dates. This, as an actual and observed case of folk-song evolution, is interesting and instructive. Two addenda verses are often sung, but as they are a kind of a tag we omit them. Mr Jas. Moir in his History of Buchan gives a version in which the narrator is of the male sex. The tune as we give it is pentatonic, and this we take to be its original character, although in many versions it is overlaid by the introduction, chiefly as passing notes, of one or both of the differentiating degrees of the scale. The tune consists of one strain, and is repeated to each quatrain. As to the introduction and position of the refrain practice varies. The song, "Barley Rigs were rakin'," is sung to a tune in 6-8 time, which is evidently akin to the tune of "Mormond Braes," which indeed I once heard sung in the same rhythm. There is another local song called "Mormond Braes" which is quite different from the present one as regards both words and music. Christie has an air of the same name, but it is different from either of the other tunes. Altogether this song is the most popular ditty which we have in Buchan. As far as I know it was first published in complete form—words and music—in my story "Logie o' Buchan," when it ran as a serial in the *Buchan Observer* some eight or nine years ago.

Our next specimen of the Buchan love song has also a connection with Strichen. As far as the results of our research show Fyvie is the favourite parish with the balladist and folk-songist, while Strichen seems to be entitled to the second place. Some parishes have failed to get their names enshrined in any songs of fairly wide vogue.

In Strichen you know.

In Strichen you know pretty plantin's do grow,
  And all things in beauty appear;
The birds on the trees sing their dearies to please,
  And the hearts of young lovers to cheer.

The houses to be seen in the middle of the green
  Most beautiful buildings appear,
Likewise the fishing pond where the small fish abound,
  Makes the hearts of young lovers to cheer.

One evening fresh and fair I went out to take the air,
  Myself to amuse for a while,
And there I did hear something tingling in mine ear,
  Which made me in silence to smile.

I drew myself on to the place where it came from
  With the softest of steps I could move,
And 'twas there I did see by the foot of a tree
  A young man embracing his love.

All in his arms twain it was there she did remain,
  While these words unto her he did say—
My dearest of all, I have got bad news to tell,
  For from you, lovey, I must away.

But, oh, he said again, I wish I could remain
  Some longer in your company, my dear,
For you're sweeter unto me than the honey to the bee,
  Or the lark in the morning to cheer.

Your cheek is like the rose that in yonder garden grows,
  And your teeth like the ivory or snow;
Your skin is white as milk, and as soft as any silk,
  Or the wool on young lambs that doth grow.

> Your love is like the moon that doth wander up and down,
>   And at every fourth quarter is new;
> But mine is like the sun in the firmament goes round,
>   And for ever proves constant and true.
>
> Like David and his clan banished from his native land,
>   Like Lazarus was slighted also,
> Which causes me to weep many a night when I should sleep,
>   My darling, for thinking on you.
>
> But here is a health, and I wish it were myself,
>   Unto those who are constant and true,
> Keeping constant and kind, never altering in mind,
>   Unto those who are constant to you.

This song raises more problems than any of the others. Like the preceding one it has been attributed to Dr Gavin, but, although something may be said for his claim to the authorship of "Mormond Braes," we are pretty sure for one reason or another that he could not have written this song, although possibly he may have adapted it in some way. In another version of the song, equally common in Buchan, we have "Forglen" in place of "Strichen." Further, verse 8 is found in "The Winter it is Past" (*Herd's MSS.*), and there are besides one or two other points in the two songs where there is a slight suggestion of kinship. "The Winter it is Past" is associated in the books with two airs (see *Museum* and Petrie's *Ancient Irish Music*), and neither is the same as the air of "In Strichen You Know"; but, strangely enough, I once heard the song in question sung to what was just a variant of our "Strichen" tune. This tune is evidently very old, and the variational range, both as to scheme and details, is unusually wide. I have noted it several times, and have examined altogether some 9 or 10 different versions. Mr Riddell has it as a Dorian, while Mr Duncan's set is Mixolydian. The variant of the tune referred to above in connection with "The Winter it is Past" was in the Dorian mode. The Mixolydian form I have noted two or three times, and about equally often I have got the form which is here given, which, beginning as a Mixolydian, passes in the latter half of the tune into the Dorian mode. In the *Folk-Song Journal*, No. 6, page 11, there is an air to different words, which, when compared with the different versions of "In Strichen You Know," would appear to have derived from the same original. Altogether, the questions connected with this song of ours—words and music, would stand some expiscation.

As I cam' in by Ythanside,
Where gently flows the rolling tide,
A bonnie lass past by my side,
Her looks did me ensnare.

This maid she was a beauty bricht
As ever trod the Braes o' Gight,
I could hae spent the lea-lang nicht
Wi' her on Ythanside.

I turned my back on Fyvie's belles,
And my poor heart gave mony a knell ;
I spiert the road to St John's Wells
With courage stout and bold.

The maid she turned without delay,
And thus to me began to say,—
I scarcely go two miles this way,
Young man, I'll tell ye plain.

But gin ye gang the gate ye cam ,
I ll get a man will show ye hame,
Oot owre yon bonny flowery glen
And hame by Ythanside.

I thanked the maid and turned right bold,
The flocks were driving to the fold,
And many a lively tale she told
Just as we passed along.

Till at length we reached her father's hame ;
Sae bashfully as I gaed ben,
Thinks I mysel', I am frae hame
Altho' on Ythanside.

But the people a' they seemed discreet,
And ilka ane aboot did creep,
The auld gudewife brought ben a seat
And bade me to sit doon.

I sat me there right weel content,
The auld gudeman for news was bent;
To view the maid was my intent,
The truth I'll tell you plain.

But the servant lads began to spit
And gather a' up to their fit;
Thinks I, My lads, ye're gaun to flit,
An' a' bound for your beds.

Then up I started straight ootricht,
And bade them a' a blythe gude-nicht,
And spiert the road to Mains o' Gight,
To which the maid replied—

I'll show you by the barn door;
Judge ye gin oor twa hearts was sore
To think we'd part to meet no more
On bonnie Ythanside.

I held the fair maid by the hand,
The time was short we had to stand,
I got a kiss upon demand;
These words to me she said—

When you come back this road again,
It's wi' you then I will be gaun;
And I gaed fustlin' through the lane,
And hame by Ythanside.

This song is pretty widely known. The words cannot be very old, and one is not astonished to find a local tradition as to their authorship. They seem to have aimed at a certain propriety of diction, and the song altogether has a "composed" look, although the local singer has begun to qualify all this by substituting here and there vernacular equivalents for the more "proper" words and phrases. The air exhibits no special characteristics. It is, both as regards rhythm and note, more smooth and flowing than folk-tunes usually are, and may have been modernised to some extent.

Folk-song with us is mostly inland and rural; but it has its points of contact with the sea and sea-faring life. The following ditty, widely popular, finds its text in an industry with which Peterhead used to be associated—seeking to exploit the romance and sentiment of the whaler's life.

Once more for Greenland we are bound,
   To leave you all behind,
With timbers firm and hearts so warm
   We sail before the wind.

We do not go to face the foe
   All on the raging main,
We only sail to catch the whale,
   But we'll soon return again.

We leave behind us on the shore
   All them we love most dear,
We leave our sweethearts and our wives
   All weeping round the pier.

Don't weep, my pretty girlies,
   Though ye be left behind ;
For the rose may bloom on Greenland's ice
   Before we change our mind.

And our wee bairnies hushed asleep,
   Their bosoms filled with pain,
Dry up your tears for one half year,
   We'll soon return again.

    .   .   .   .   .   .

Now at last we've reached the ice,
   And quickly crowd our sail ;
Each boat we'll man wi' a good band
   For to pursue the whale.

Now homewards we are bound again,
   And pass the Orkney Isles ;
A flowing cup raised to our lips,
   Which does the time beguile.

And now the shore appears in view,
  The steamboat she draws near,
We see our sweethearts and our wives
  All waiting round the pier.

To Greenland's frost we'll drink a toast,
  To them we love most dear;
Across the main to it again
  We'll take a trip next year.

The air is a well-known one, and is sung to other folk-ditties, such as "Young Ellen of Aberdeen," and "Jean o' Bannermill." From its cadence one would adjudge it Irish, a conclusion which is strengthened by the fact that Petrie gives it in his *Ancient Irish Music* (No. 790). His version of the tune has two strains. I have noted it a number of times (to different words), but always as a one-strain melody. Mr Riddell, however, has a version of this song with a second strain, needing eight lines to complete the stanza.

We would now submit one or two specimens of the local Ploughman Song.—

As I gaed in by Netherdale
  At Turra market for to fee,
I met in wi' a fairmer chap
  Frae the Barnyards o' Delgaty.
    Liltrin adie toorin adie,
    Liltrin adie tooral ee.

He promised me the ae best pair
  I'd ever set my een upon;
When I gaed hame to the Barnyards
  There was naething there but skin and bone.

The auld black horse sat on his rump,
  The auld white mear lay on her wime,
And a' that I could hup and crack,
  They wadna rise at yokin' time.

Meg Macpherson mak's my brose,
  But her and me we canna gree,
First a mote and syne a knot,
  And aye the tither jilp o' bree.

But yet when I gang to the kirk,
  Mony's the bonnie lass I see,
Prim sittin' by her daddy's side,
  And winkin' owre the pews to me.

I can drink and nae be drunk,
  I can fight and nae be slain,
I can coort anither's lass,
  And aye be welcome to my ain.

My can'le noo it is brunt oot,
  The snotter's fairly on the wane;
Sae fare ye weel, ye Barnyards,
  Ye'll never catch me here again.

We have already dealt pretty fully with our Ploughman Songs on the side of the words, and it may be enough to say here that the versions vary chiefly as to extent and completeness. Being as a rule just a series of characterisations and experiences the songs can easily take on addenda verses, and as easily on the other hand can they bear curtailment. There are usually one or two *in camera* verses. The air of this song is one of our most popular folk-tunes, and is associated with several other ditties, the refrain being always common property. It is pentatonic, and only once or twice have we got it with a passing *te* or *fa* which some modern singer had introduced. The most corrupt version we have seen is that given in "Songs of the North."

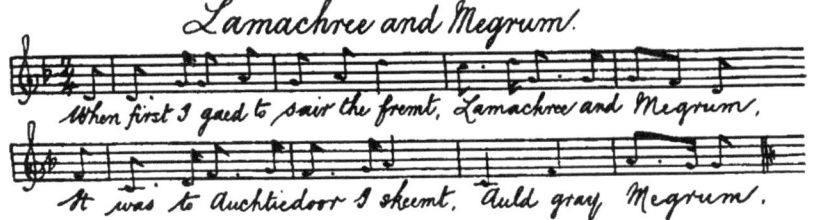

When first I gaed to sair the fremt,
  Lamachree and Megrum,
It was to Auchtiedoor I skeemt,
  Auld gray Megrum.

The auld gudewife smokes in the neuk,
　　Lamachree and Megrum,
A orderin' at the throw'ther cook,
　　Auld gray Megrum.

The neist, I gaed to Middlethird,
　　Lamachree and Megrum,
A better's nae abeen the yird,
　　Auld gray Megrum.

I there got buttered breid and cheese,
　　Lamachree and Megrum,
And oil to keep my sheen in grease,
　　Auld gray Megrum.

I took a turn at Yokieshill,
　　Lamachree and Megrum,
The teuchest place I e'er gaed till,
　　Auld gray Megrum.

A hurb to hack and hash the loons,
　　Lamachree and Megrum,
There's nae his like in Buchan's boun's,
　　Auld gray Megrum.

A song like this can go on indefinitely. We have heard "Mains o' Culsh" sung to the same tune with the same enigmatical refrain. The air is a Dorian, with a tendency to mix the modes.

Cameloun.

It's Tarves pairish that I come frae,
And to tell ye that I am some wae,
For there's ae lang road that I maun gae,
　　To the Fyvie lands in the mornin'.

At Cameloun I did arrive,
A pair o' horses for to drive,
And ilka morn to rise at five,
　　And ca the fan in the mornin'.

I hadna weel begun to sleep
When the foreman he began to creep,
And oot o's bed he sprang till's feet—
 Cries, Losh boys, rise, for it's mornin'.

To ca the fan they set me tee,
Which I began richt cannily,
And took a look hoo they wid dee
 In the Fyvie lands in the mornin'.

We hae a bailie stoot and stark,
It sets him weel to work his wark,
But owre his heid he's drawn a sark,
 As lang's himsel' in the mornin'.

The winnyin' bein' past and the fan by set,
The foreman says, We maun hae mate, [meat]
At the heid o' the table he's ta'en his seat,
 Sayin', Ate boys, ate, for it's mornin'.

Ye'll yoke yer horse as fast's ye may,
The foreman unto me did say,
Ye'll get a pleuchie oot owre the brae
 That'll please ye weel in the mornin'.

I hadna lang been at the ploo
When I began to couck and spew,
The nicht afore I'd been some fou,
 Sae I had a dowie mornin'.

 .   .   .   .

He said I didna my horses ken,
And on me he laid a' the blame,
But I loot him ken I'd been frae hame,
 In the Fyvie lands in the mornin'.

It's I ca'd him a stupid ass,
Bade him come forrit wi' my brass,
And awa' frae his toon I'd tak' my pass
 Wi' richt guidwill in the mornin'.

Fyvie pairish is lang and wide,
Fyvie pairish is fu' o' pride,
But in this cauld corner I'll nae langer bide
 Gin I had Whitsunday mornin'.

The tune, which we have got associated with another song, is a Dorian, with some of its interval softened by the introduction of passing notes. The last line of the melody lends itself to bucolic intonation and inflection more perfectly than any other succession of notes which we have ever come across in folk-tune.

O Charlie, O Charlie, come owre frae Pitgair,
  And I'll gie ye oot a' your orders,
For I maun awa' to the high hielan hills,
  For a while to leave the bonnie Buchan borders.

O Charlie, O Charlie, tak' notice what I say,
  And pit every man to his station,
For I'm gaun awa' to the high hielan hills,
  For to view a' the pairts o' the nation.

To the lowsin' ye'll pit Shaw, ye'll pit Sandieson to ca,
  To the colin' ye'll pit auld Andrew Kindness,
Ye'll gar auld Colliehill aye feed the thrashin' mill,
  And ye'll see that he dee't wi' great fineness.

To the gatherin' o' the hay ye'll pit little Isa Gray,
  And wi' her ye'll pit her cousin Peggie,
And in below the bands it's there ye'll pit your hands,
  And ye'll see that they dee it richt tidy.

And for you, Willie Burr, ye'll cairry on the stir,
  And ye'll keep a' the lassies a-hyowin',
And ye'll tak' care o' Jeck, or he'll play ye a trick,
  And set a your merry maids a-mowin'.

> And for you, Annie Scott, ye'll pit on the muckle pot,
>   And ye'll mak' to them pottage in plenty.
> For yon hungry brosers that's comin' frae Pitgair
>   They're keepit aye sae bare and scanty.
>
> O Charlie, O Charlie, sae early's ye'll rise,
>   And see a' my merry men yokin',
> And you, Missy Pope, ye'll sit in the parlour neuk,
>   And keep a' my merry men frae smokin'.

Pitgair is a farm in the parish of Gamrie. The song, unsurpassed among local pastorals for simplicity and truth, is said to have been written by a man named Shaw, who was long beadle at Alvah, and had considerable local reputation as a rhymer. We do not as a rule set much store by traditions as to authorship. When they merely give us the name of a man otherwise unknown, even should the information be true, we have got *vox et praeterea nihil*. But Shaw is credited with other local songs, such as "Mrs Greig of Sandlaw" and "Lucky Duff." The air does duty for several other songs and ballads, and belongs to a type very common in this part of the country. We consider it one of the most beautiful of our traditional melodies, the cadences being particularly fine. In general outline it bears some resemblance to "My love's in Germany."

A crisis has come in the history of our folk-songs. The attention of the cultured world has been drawn to them. They are being collected, edited, printed. Their primitive strains are being reduced to conventional notation and clothed with up-to-date instrumental accompaniments. We need not trouble to point out how difficult it is to write accompaniments for modal tunes—difficult in the case of Dorians and Aeolians, almost impossible in the case of Mixolydians; nor need we stay to pity the plight of our poor Pentatonics as the pianoforte pelts them with the notes which they have forsworn. These are details. The main and significant fact remains that the wildings are being dressed and decked for good society. The "bird of the wilderness" has been caught, put in a gilded cage and hung up in the drawing-room. Will it —can it now sing as it did in its wild freedom, "when upward springing blithe to greet the purpling east?" In plain terms can folk-song survive and yield its message in these new and strange conditions?

Some of our traditional ditties will pass upward into a class above true folk-song, to reinforce and enrich our national minstrelsy. But the many will pine and die "with the burden of an honour unto which they were not born." Whence then this seemingly ill-advised and fatal interest in folk-song? Why not leave it alone? Had things been going on in the old way it would certainly have been better to leave it alone. But a crisis has come. Like the aboriginal races before the white man folk-song is dying out before the march of education and the advance of musical culture. Hence the appearance on the scene of the litterateur and musician. The collector's note-book and the engraver's plates are indeed lethal instruments; but when folk-song is seen to be *in extremis* it has been judged better to have it die in our hands so that we may at least keep and embalm the poor remains, than to let it flutter off into the wild or crawl into the thicket, there to die unseen, and perish quite from off the face of the earth.—Such aim has the folk-song collector; and such is his justification.

1

Lightning Source UK Ltd.
Milton Keynes UK
UKHW021820020220
358029UK00003B/372